'In this book Jane brings the vast amount of evidence and research together in a way that is compelling and accessible, drawing on her areas of expertise including health behaviour, prevention and sexual violence.'

Claire Bloor,
CEO SARSAS (Somerset and Avon Rape and Sexual Abuse Support).

'Sexual abuse happens in communities by members of those communities against each other, and therefore it is our responsibility as members of communities to be aware of the reality of sexual abuse so that we can safety intervene to prevent it from occurring. Which is why this book is so important; we need to talk about sexual abuse to understand it and combat it, which means presenting the evidence base in an informed and accessible way.'

Kieran McCartan,
Professor of Criminology.

'Where prevention work has been done it has not covered a range of forms of violence; for example it has focused more often on domestic violence and less so on other forms, such as sexual harassment, stalking or crimes of "honour". Jane Meyrick has reviewed some key initiatives in this publication.'

Purna Sen,
ex-UN Women Policy Lead, Visiting Professor CWSAU (London Metropolitan University).

#MeToo for Women and Men

#MeToo for Women and Men provides an overview of sexual violence and an accessible guide to the #MeToo movement, presenting a timely look at the evidence from diverse fields. Its evidence-based approach builds upon public health and health psychology principles to increase the reader's understanding of sexual bullying and aims to help inform the building of safer communities.

The book identifies patterns of sexual harassment and considers how sexual bullying can be used to express power. Intended to widen readers' knowledge of the causes and impacts surrounding sexual harassment and abuse, the book encourages open discussion of these topics to enable society to move closer to combating it. Using first-person accounts alongside evidence of both individual behaviours and the ways the topic is dealt with in laws, institutions, cultures and organisations, the book ensures that voices of survivors and their experiences are emphasised throughout.

A wide audience of public, professional, academics and clinicians will benefit from the book's extensive look into the impact sexual harassment has on survivors and its insight into how connections across a range of fields help us to understand, but more importantly, prevent perpetration and victimisation. This guide is also for non-academics wanting to understand what #MeToo means, what it tells us about prevention and how to address the increasing problem of sexual harassment, violence and abuse.

Jane Meyrick is both a chartered health psychologist and a public health specialist. She has been working in and researching sexual health for over 25 years. Her career spans frontline sexual health services, national policy and research. She has been teaching health psychology since 2006 at the University of the West of England, Bristol, UK.

#MeToo for Women and Men

Understanding Power through Sexual Harassment

Jane Meyrick

Routledge
Taylor & Francis Group

LONDON AND NEW YORK

Cover image: © Rafael Graf / EyeEm / Getty Images

First published 2022
by Routledge
4 Park Square, Milton Park, Abingdon, Oxon OX14 4RN

and by Routledge
605 Third Avenue, New York, NY 10158

Routledge is an imprint of the Taylor & Francis Group, an informa business

British Library Cataloguing-in-Publication Data
A catalogue record for this book is available from the British Library

Library of Congress Cataloging-in-Publication Data
Names: Meyrick, Jane, author.
Title: #MeToo for women and men : understanding power through sexual harassment / Jane Meyrick.
Description: Abingdon, Oxon ; New York, NY : Routledge, 2022. | Includes bibliographical references and index.
Identifiers: LCCN 2021057890 (print) | LCCN 2021057891 (ebook) | ISBN 9780367767976 (paperback) | ISBN 9780367767983 (hardback) | ISBN 9781003168591 (ebook)
Subjects: LCSH: Sex crimes. | Sexual harassment. | Sexual abuse victims. | Control (Psychology)
Classification: LCC HV6556 .M49 2022 (print) | LCC HV6556 (ebook) | DDC 364.15/3—dc23/eng/20220302
LC record available at https://lccn.loc.gov/2021057890
LC ebook record available at https://lccn.loc.gov/2021057891

ISBN: 978-0-367-76798-3 (hbk)
ISBN: 978-0-367-76797-6 (pbk)
ISBN: 978-1-003-16859-1 (ebk)

DOI: 10.4324/9781003168591

Typeset in Bembo
by Apex CoVantage, LLC

Contents

RAPE CRISIS
England & Wales

Rape Crisis England & Wales is the umbrella body for a network of independent Rape Crisis Centres. All member Centres provide specialist support and services for victims and survivors of sexual violence.

Available: Open between 12:00–14:30 and 19:00–21:30 every day of the year.
Telephone: 0808 802 9999.
Website: rapecrisis.org.uk/get-help/want-to-talk/. One to One live chat Helpline

SURVIVORSUK
male rape and sexual abuse

Survivors UK

Survivors UK offers a range of support services including counselling and therapy appointments as well as online chat. All services are provided by trained professionals who as specialists in the field of male sexual violence have helped many men to work through their experiences.

Available: Mon–Fri 09:30–17:00 (office hours)
Mon–Sun 12:00–20:00 (helpline web chat)
Telephone: 0203 598 3898
e-mail: help@survivorsuk.org
Website: SurvivorsUK | We challenge the silence to support sexually abused men

Helps with: male sexual assault, male rape

Galop UK

Galop provides confidential and independent advice and support for LGBT+ people who have experienced sexual assault, abuse or violence.

Available: Mon–Fri 10:00–17:00
　　　　　　　Wed–Thu 10:00–20:00
Telephone: 0800 999 5428
e-mail: help@galop.org.uk
Website: Galop – The LGBT+ anti-violence charity

Helps with: LGBT sexual assault, domestic abuse, violence

Southall Black Sisters
A group of black and minority women providing a comprehensive service to women experiencing violence and abuse.

Available: Mon–Fri 09:00–17:00
Telephone: 0208 571 9595
Website: https://southallblacksisters.org.uk/contact-us/

Helps with: sexual violence, domestic abuse, forced marriage

About the author

Jane Meyrick is a Chartered Health Psychologist (Associate Fellow of the british psychology society, Health and Care Professions Council registered) and a Public Health Specialist (Fellow of the Faculty of Public Health and UKPHR registered). She has been working and researching sexual health for over 25 years encompassing sex education, sexual healthcare and sexual violence. She brings together the understanding of experiences and behaviour from psychology with the tools of public health in epidemiological data, evidence, cause and effect from society to the individual.

Her teaching and research within health psychology focuses on the less heard voices within sexual health including survivors of sexual abuse and violence. She works closely with local NHS sexual health services and specialist sexual violence counselling agencies. She has extensive experience in service delivery roles including sex education/health programmes and research and also in national and regional policymaking and practice.

Acknowledgements

To those who let me listen and represent their stories, I hope the voice of your experiences can be heard in this book. Thank you.

To those who do the support and research work against overwhelming odds, thank you for your wisdom and hard work.

To those who let me write, my sons and my partner, thank you.

To those who let me endlessly rehearse my reasoning, my friends, thank you.

Foreword

Claire Bloor,
CEO, Somerset and Avon Rape and Sexual Abuse Support

The first time I experienced sexual harassment three men in their 30s 'curb crawled' alongside me while shouting obscenities. I was 11 years old, and I was in my school uniform. Sadly, this wasn't novel or unusual, it had happened to many of the girls at primary school already, but it was frightening and it felt like an early life lesson in who held the power in society. Twenty-seven years later when the #MeToo movement, started by Tarana Burke and reinvigorated in 2017 by Alyssa Milano, gathered steam I reflected again on how my experiences of sexual harassment and abuse mirrored those of so many women I knew and those I didn't who were now coming forward and declaring it en masse. It felt horrifying to see such widespread abuse laid bare but also invigorating to hear the roar of women saying enough is enough.

It was no coincidence that the following year, after 25 years in the charity sector, I took my current role of Chief Executive Officer at SARSAS (Somerset and Avon Rape and Sexual Abuse Support): an incredible charity that supports those impacted by rape and sexual abuse to heal and recover and campaigns for an end to sexual violence and to ensure no one is left unheard. I was suddenly plunged into the world of sexual violence statistics – at least one in five women will experience some form of sexual violence at some time in their lives; less than 15% of victim-survivors will report their abuse; less than 2% of those accused will be convicted. In my role I saw that we supported over 5000 women and girls and men and boys a year. I heard how our helpline calls had increased by over 250% following the child sexual abuse of Jimmy Saville being exposed and how we were seeing a new spike related to #MeToo. I could see how victim-survivors would find the courage to come forward after days, months or even years to ask for help only to be told that they had to wait, often for a year or more, as demand for support in our organisation and across the sector massively exceeded our funded capacity to deliver services. I saw the perniciousness of rape myths and victim blaming and their impact on those who have experienced sexual violence and on our culture and community. And as I tried to learn about the sector, I could see that there were vast amounts of research and evidence but that much of it was inaccessible and hard to make sense of.

It was through the partnership work of SARSAS and the University of Western England, considering how best to support victim-survivors of sexual violence on university campuses and deliver training and support around enthusiastic consent to students, that I met Jane. Jane is an incredible advocate for victim-survivors and for specialist sexual violence services, always looking at partnership opportunities to ensure best practice, researched and evidenced work.

In this book Jane brings the vast amount of evidence and research together in a way that is compelling and accessible, drawing on her areas of expertise including health behaviour, prevention and sexual violence. Through this work you can get a sense of the scope and breadth of sexual violence and Jane provides a language that allows you to understand it. She makes the connections between male power and the cultural structures that have allowed sexual violence to thrive along with the effect and impact. The most powerful part of this for me is the voice of victim-survivors that comes through so strongly in the quotes, it allows you to really hear that impact and understand it. As Jane says later, 'Hearing victim-survivor testimony may produce a much needed cultural shift in visibility and greater understanding of the life-long impact of experiencing sexual abuse/violence'. At SARSAS we see this in practice every day, along with the impact of rape myths and victim blaming that aim to silence and shame victim-survivors who feel like their experiences are shrouded in darkness. Our role is to shine a light and support survivors to speak, then to listen and believe them. As we know, there can be no shame where there is empathy and light.

So how far have we really come since #MeToo? It definitely started a long over-due public conversation allowing people to see how prevalent and harmful sexual harassment and abuse is. It outed the cultural normalisation of sexual harassment and abuse. And in some ways the narrative has changed as a result. But that change has not been swift or decisive enough and we have felt the inevitable #MeToo backlash and the rise of the #NotAllMen 'debate'!

We still live in a culture where men take and women are available to be taken, summarised in the quote Jane uses from The Children's Commissioner: 'too many boys believe that they have an absolute entitlement to sex at any time, in any place, in any way and with whomever they wish. Equally worryingly, we heard that too often girls feel they have no alternative but to submit to boys' demands, regardless of their own wishes' (1). This has been seen writ large in the 2021 OFSTED Report highlighting the normalisation of sexual harassment in schools and the Everyone's Invited website that uses testimonies of survivors to call out rape culture in schools. In the week of writing this (July 2021) alone we have seen the reports of appalling rates of sexual violence in the military and child sexual abuse in the Scouts.

The research and evidence Jane considered in the chapter on prevention shows programmes need to be funded and delivered and we need to keep challenging the rape myths and culture that allow sexual violence to flourish. We also need to sustainably fund services for victim-survivors so that when they are ready to seek the support and help they deserve, that support is readily available.

Foreword

Kieran McCartan,
Professor of Criminology,
University of the West of England

Sexual abuse is present in every culture and country on the planet; it is, unfortunately, not abnormal, or unique. It is something present in our communities and often, both directly and indirectly, in our homes. Most people know at least one person, often more, that have been impacted by sexual abuse. Which means that sexual abuse is not something that happens to other people, it is something that happens to us and people we care about. People who commit sexual abuse, like those impacted by it, come from communities, and return to communities after the abuse has occurred. Therefore, it is essential that the public at large have a realistic understanding of sexual abuse, its causes and consequences. Unfortunately, the public do not have a realistic understanding of sexual abuse, they have an understanding polluted by misperceptions, stereotypes and misdirection. But where have these lapses in understanding come from? The press, media and social media? Friends, family and peers? Poor processing and cognitive distortions? Ignorance and lack of engagement? Yes, all of the above and more! To understand sexual abuse, we need to confront the issue face on and have the difficult conversation and address the reality of the situation.

It's debatable if the conversation about sexual abuse has moved forward in the last 100 years or whether it has just become more visible. The advent of the #MeToo movement brought the conversation of sexual abuse to a new generation, we have been here every decade since the 1960s, with the hope that this time we could raise the profile and eradicate sexual abuse forever. Can we? The jury is still out! But what we have seen is a broader discussion of the reality of sexual abuse, conversations about experiences of sexual abuse, an openness to develop effective sexual abuse prevention strategies, and to really think about what victims want in their recovery from sexual abuse. The #MeToo movement highlighted the individualised nature of sexual abuse and emphasised that each victim/survivor wanted something different from their decision to disclose whether that was be to be heard, to seek justice, or to offer support to others. This is vital, as it pushed back against the ideal that all victims are homogenous and then therefore raised the question of – are we really helping victims with the support that we offer or are we offering support that appeases us? In doing this the #MeToo movement highlighted the complexity of sexual abuse, it showed that abuse is not one dimensional and that the relationship (or relationships) between victim and preparator can change. Additionally, what this has done is high-light that people who commit abuse, or preparators, are not one dimensional themselves. They commit sexual abuse for several reasons, which means that the traditional misguided stereotype of what a child abuser, rapist and pae-dophile is is not fit for purposes because people who commit sexual abuse can look like and be anyone. Context can change the nature of behaviour and, therefore, the same person can act in different ways in different situa-tions. However, in saying this there are aspects of behavioural consistency that travel across contexts, but some contexts make them more pronounced. There are behaviours and actions that we can look out for, warning signs or triggers, that make the prevention of sexual abuse more likely. As stated before, sexual abuse happens in communities by members of those commu-nities against each other, and therefore it is our responsibility as members of communities to be aware of the reality of sexual abuse so that we can safely intervene to prevent it from occurring.

Which is why this book is so important; we need to talk about sexual abuse to understand it and combat it, which means presenting the evidence base in an informed and accessible way.

Foreword

Purna Sen,
ex-UN Women Policy Lead, Visiting Professor
CWSAU (London Metropolitan University)

It's just part of life, of work; it's what happens when we go out, are on a train or bus or are at university. Unwanted comments, touches, looks as well as assault and rape enter the consciousness of women and girls at an early age but endure whole lifetimes, as we are taught these are risks and everyday threats against which females the world over must guard. And guard we do: by modifying our dress, movements, words and actions.

Everyday women and girls curtail their freedoms and forego their full humanity so that the abuse meted out them by men (and fear of it) is not only anticipated and avoided but additionally in the hope that blame for that abuse is not visited upon them.

UNEQUAL LIVES

Cost-free male sexual access to women is at the core of cultural norms that reflect and uphold gender inequality. These build distrust of, and undermine, women's knowledge and value more highly men's voices, expectations and lives. Sexual violence and other sexual harassment are not random acts by aberrant men but patterns of behaviour that shape our worlds in sometimes invisible yet tangible and powerful ways. Sexual violence and sexual harassment express male sexual entitlement, in particular to the bodies of women and girls. They are premised on various axes of inequality – sex and gender dominant among them – but persistent dimensions include minoritised status such as race, ethnicity, disability, sexual orientation and indigeneity.

Meaningful and impactful prevention efforts need to recognise and contest these inequalities. They need to build upon and promote the full humanity of women and girls. That means fully valuing women's bodies, lives and futures rather than treating these as somehow lesser than those of men or as cheap collateral for male benefit.

RESPONDING VS PREVENTING

Women have long craved a world where there is no violence – its reality and threat limits, harms and ends too many lives. In 2015, states across the world formally reflected this vision, evidenced in their commitment to eliminate all forms of violence against women and children by 2030 (2).

Progressing elimination requires a broader view and range of actions than responding to abuse through a focus on the abused. It can be impactful only if there is recognition that violence against women, including and beyond sexual harassment, involves patterns not aberrations and that elimination requires not only responses but prevention.

What if we were to understand that violence against women is not simply about a few bad apples, aberrant people (predominantly men) who are 'psychologically unwell' or in other ways deemed at odds with their social environment? What if we understood that in fact those who abuse, violate, rape, sexually harass or otherwise abuse women and girls, are actually in sync with the messages that infuse the contexts in which we all operate? Then we would have to look further than fixing broken individuals to addressing large-scale cultural and structural issues.

WHAT DOES PREVENTION LOOK LIKE?

It is said that there is a limited evidence base about what works to prevent abuse and that the bulk of this work is in the global south – what the UN and development agencies/funders tend to refer to as developing or low- and middle-income countries. Additionally, where prevention work has been done it has not covered a range of forms of violence; for example it has focused more often on domestic violence and less so on other forms, such as sexual harassment, stalking or crimes of 'honour'. Jane Meyrick has reviewed some key initiatives in this publication.

A recent international framework (2) acknowledges that it draws on intimate partner violence and non-partner sexual assault work and sets out these elements of prevention work:

- Preventing violence before it occurs – no 'new cases' of violence
- Preventing the recurrence of violence: addressing re-victimisation and stopping men re-abusing
- Preventing or limiting the impacts of Violence Against Women through short- and long-term care and support.

Each of these rests on a foundation in which social norms are addressed. No one area of work can have adequate or lasting impact in isolation – this makes prevention work complex and perhaps daunting to some. Limited prevention initiatives can be seen as problematic, making it hard to know what efforts bring lasting behavioural change. Are initiatives in the global south replicable elsewhere? Unfortunately, transferability is limited by framing violence against women as an issue of under-development, crisis or other circumstances related to linked concerns such as poverty or poor governance.

For prevention to be effective it must at the least

- Have a long-term vision amongst all those involved in this work, including funders.
- Undo dominant gender norms that uphold men as sexually entitled beings and women and girls as sexually submissive and available; this includes addressing the sex industry's role in perpetuating and escalating the normalisation of sexualised violence.
- Name and redress the ways in which different women's bodies are valued, sexualised and commodified not least of all by ablism and histories of empire and slavery. This work has to be led by the knowledge and wisdom of those on the frontlines.
- Fulfil the rights of women and girls to freedom from violence, and its threat, by states, communities and the organisations in which we operate.

These are the minimalist elements that will move us away from the constant 'safety work' (3) done by women and girls towards a time and place where freedom and joy are known.

REFERENCES

(1) See targets 5.2, 5.3 and 16.2 https://sdgs.un.org/goals/goal5
(2) www.unwomen.org/-/media/headquarters/attachments/sections/library/publications/2015/prevention_framework_unwomen_nov2015.pdf?la=en&vs=5223
(3) Vera-Gray, F., & Kelly, L. (2020). Contested gendered space: Public sexual harassment and women's safety work. In *Crime and Fear in Public Places* (pp. 217–231). Routledge.

Introduction

We should aim for a society that allows young people to choose a life, not constrained by artificial gender stereotypes and free from gender-driven social policing – girls not defined in sexual currency, men free to nurture. Most people do not make the connection between gender stereotypes and sexual abuse and harassment. That is where data and evidence come in. We can look across patterns, connections and causes to find a way to prevention.

> "I knew him. He was my best friend's cousin. I didn't know any better and IT WASN'T THE FIRST TIME HE ASSAULTED ME. Have I told anyone this until now? No! Why? Because I knew no one would believe me #MeToo."
>
> (2)

These are the words of just one victim/survivor telling their story via the only platform she saw as willing to witness it, the Twitter handle #MeToo.

Tarana Burker and Alyssa Milano used the phrase #MeToo to tell the world that they had heard and recognised the stories of high profile victim/survivors of sexual abuse because it had happened to them as well (3). This Twitter movement became a moment for many to echo their own similar stories and in so doing, call out the pandemic proportions of sexual harassment and abuse (3). It built on previous scaffolding of 'ethical witnessing' (4) and captured a place that broke through the silence surrounding women's widespread common victimisation. Testimony ranges from posting an acknowledgement of experiences of sexual harassment with a simple #MeToo, through to detailed sharing of full accounts (3). Up to 34 million Twitter users may have seen such first-person revelations from someone they followed or knew just in the first week of the movement (3). Since then it has become shorthand for experiences of sexual harassment and abuse and yet the voices we hear more often are those concerned about the accused (5).

DOI: 10.4324/9781003168591-1

"Men have had their careers and reputations ruined overnight by #MeToo – some possibly justly, but without any due process, no innocence until proven guilty." (Jessica Butcher, Equalities Minster)

(6)

Critics of #MeToo cite the lack of due process in using public naming as a means of redress (6). My question is, why do these survivors feel this is the only way they can speak of their trauma? We should try to understand the meaning behind #MeToo as well as listen to the voices of those trying to live with the impact of the sexual abuse they suffered. This has become more urgent as new examples of online testimony have shown, that for women and girls in the UK, (7) live with an ignored 'rape culture' in schools and universities.

At the heart of this book are the words of those who have experienced what we are addressing; a wide range of victim/survivors' accounts are used to give meaning, including testimony to select committees, participants in the author's own research and reported quotes from published research studies. At the heart of #MeToo lies the feeling that there is nowhere else to tell and no one else to listen.

CHAPTER 1

#MeToo is everywhere – scale

*"It does happen a lot, but people don't think much of it anymore.
It's just like 'Oh, that's happened again'. People just kind of accept it."*

(8)

It feels like sexual harassment is everywhere; many women say that low-level harassment is such an everyday event that they barely register it anymore (9). I am writing about all sexual harassment wherever it takes place, in public spaces, in the workplace, in schools, in universities and online and I am talking about the full range of sexual bullying, from wolf whistle to rape. Much of the shock around the online collation of women's experiences that is #MeToo, was the revelation (something most women knew from personal experience) that it was in fact common to so many. For many men, the shock was how many women they knew posted #MeToo (10). For others it was the silence from workplaces, educational providers, the police, friends and family where it takes place.

"I would not have reported any of the incidents that I experienced to
the police because I did not think that I would be taken seriously or that
there was anything that the police could do."

(11)

Most sexual violence is hidden and most victim/survivors remain silent (12). Let's face it, in the wake of Dr Christine Blasey-Ford's courageous testimony to the US Supreme Courts confirmation hearing (13),

"I am here today not because I want to be: I am terrified. I am here
because I believe it is my civic duty to tell you what happened to me
while Brett Kavanaugh and I were in high school."

(14)

DOI: 10.4324/9781003168591-2

and the personal cost to her,

> "The reality has been far worse than what I expected. My family and I have been the target of constant harassment and death threats and I've been called the most vile and hateful names imaginable."
>
> (14)

Why would you report the abuse? It is hard to see any benefit to Dr Blasey-Ford beyond her own sense of duty. If even an articulate, white, privileged victim/survivor's account is met with disbelief and death threats, keeping quiet seems the safer option.

Research survey data confirms that internationally around 80–90% of women report ever having experienced sexual harassment (9,15–19). This includes around 80% in the UK with 97% (almost all) of young women aged 18–24 reporting a range of sexual harassment in public (9). Statistics are based on different ways of framing the question so what is recorded varies (20). The often cited figure of one in three women victimised, originally published by the WHO (21), wraps up physical violence, non-partner and intimate partner sexual violence but does not include sexual harassment or stalking. More in-depth questions return levels reaching 'almost all' (9).

The most visible form, street sexual harassment, seems to be a statement, a loud, shouted statement, of how women are valued by their appearance and attractiveness. It is experienced at different levels in different places but forms part of what can be described as a 'continuum of objectification' (22). For many, it was only hearing or reading other women tell their stories through #MeToo that allowed them to recognise what had happened to them was not okay (23). Men do also experience sexual harassment, abuse and violence but perhaps not on the same scale or scope, nor is it supported by systemic inequality.

This continuum of objectification of women and the way it is experienced as an escalating scale of violence makes it hard to highlight individual acts from the background noise or cumulative effect of constant harassment (24). Importantly, it connects the 'milder' forms of sexual bullying such as cat calling or wolf whistling directly to the threat of sexual assault or violence (22). One is a direct reminder of the possibility of the other and that women are not safe and that they are a sexual object. 'Nice arse' shouted from a passing car could be translated as, 'I own this space'.

> "It's also like, is sexualised street harassment a gateway? If you're that type of person where you're gonna say that, what would you do to me in a dark alley?"
>
> (8)

Let's consider the scope of what that sexual violence means for women and girls. It is linked to the everyday experiences of sexual harassment in the street but also abuse at work and Intimate Partner Violence (IPV) in their relationships. Eleven years of UK homicide records show that on average 5.7% (296 total) of male homicide victims and 44.2% (1066) of female homicide victims are killed by a partner or ex-partner. From 2009 to 2018, at least 1,425 women were killed by men in the UK; every three days a woman is killed by a man and every four days by a man who was her partner or ex-partner.

> "Women who are killed are most likely to have been killed by a man, men who are killed are most likely to have been killed by a man."
>
> (25)

The problem with most of the work around prevalence, or how much sexual abuse/harassment goes on, is agreeing what it is we are measuring (20). At one end, crucial work of the Femicide Census collates easily recognisable data on how many women are killed by men (generally current or ex-partners) not collated elsewhere (26). Most people would be able to describe sexual assault or rape as doing something sexual to someone without their consent, but 'just a hand on the knee' has been used to excuse or minimise even high-profile incidents (27). Controversy often arises around the more ambiguous behaviours that make up 'lower-level' sexual harassment. This book covers the full spectrum with recognition that for most women and especially for those with previous experience of sexual abuse, even so-called 'minor incidents' speak directly to potential greater harm.

WHAT DOES SEXUAL HARASSMENT/BULLYING LOOK LIKE?

As soon as definitions come into the frame, views tend to polarise around what actions 'mean' (27); is 'a hand on the knee' a compliment or a threat? This in turn makes studying sexual bullying fraught with disagreement about what constitutes harassment or rape (28). The missing piece is how these acts were 'meant/intended' or 'felt/experienced'. 'Alright love' can be expressed to mean 'shut up' or 'how are you'.

> "I shout back 'Keep dreaming.' He answers back, telling me to 'steady on' and he calls me 'love'."
>
> (29)

It is something that can range across; interruptions by male strangers; verbal intrusions; sexualised language ('just a compliment' but also abusive such as 'slut'); non-verbal intrusion (staring/following, leering blocking) through to overt sexual behaviour (22). Often, it is the mundanity of the behaviour that causes women problems in working out what happened let alone reporting it or having it taken seriously (30). Why shouldn't 'give us a smile' equal just being friendly? Because you are a stranger, this is public space and you would not say the same thing to another bloke, it is an intrusion (31).

> "A few seconds later, he was standing next to me so he had run and followed me. He walked with me as I politely told him to 'go away'. He asked where I was from and said I was being rude. He asked where I was going and I just said I was shopping and again told him to go away. He said he was going the same way as me so he decided to walk with me."
>
> (32)

The majority (61% of men and 52% of women) of both sexes feel it is always/usually wrong for men to make unsolicited comments to women in public places and the younger or more educated you are, the more you hold that view (33). However, women and girls are taught to play down their own instincts and address their own behaviour when it happens (31).

Even small acts of intrusion are described by Dr Pam Lowe as 'breaking the rule of civil inattention' where you show you are aware of others (such as moving aside) but do not otherwise engage with them, unless they are a woman to whom even 'polite intrusions' manifest as harassment (34).

It follows that work to report and prosecute such behaviour is undermined by difficulties in definition. Recipients of such behaviour will talk about it feeling 'creepy' and it is important to recognise the role of non-verbal communication (35). It is often neglected in the field of sexual harassment and consent, dominated as it is by legal and therefore, concrete efforts to evidence an offence.

> "The offence was deemed as suspicious circumstance as opposed to assault as the man brushed against me as opposed to pinching me (that apparently was the difference). I was terrified of going home that night – convinced that I was being followed. I lived alone and was frightened of being home and frightened of going out too. I changed my behaviours and began walking beside or behind other women or families so that I wouldn't be alone."
>
> (36)

Despite the problems with contested forms of evidence, the legal definition of sexual harassment focuses on how the targeted person feels and how the harassing behaviour was experienced (37). We will focus later on experiences of sexual violence/abuse and the harm of acts of perpetration for the victim/survivor, in Chapter 4, for now we need to understand the impact of widespread but mundane levels of sexual harassment.

WHAT DOES SEXUAL HARASSMENT/BULLYING FEEL LIKE?

That nature of sexual harassment or behaviour that feels intrusive resists tight definition but is different from normal social interaction in both the intruder's intention and victim's experience of being made to feel uncomfortable or 'creeped out' (38).

Some reframing of acts of perpetration has come about through the introduction, in some parts of the UK, of misogynistic hate crime. This is based on the Macpherson definitions of a racist incident (39), so 'what is the perception, harm and impact' rather than who did or said what. The category requires the police to consider the experience from the point of view of the person to whom the behaviour was directed. Eleven police forces have been using misogynistic hate crime which extends to 'being catcalled, whistled at or stopped for conversation by men who make me uncomfortable' (8). The evidence base for this work is not yet strong enough to prove any benefit and evaluation work points to a lack of communication about the changes that means most women don't know about what role hate crime can play until they come to actually report it (8). The role of laws may be in communicating awareness of what sexual harassment constitutes and what is or is not legal (40).

Attempts to focus more on the victims' perspective through terms such as 'unwanted behaviour' may have more meaning and can include the context of the situation and non-verbal behaviour (41). Others say this shifts the burden to victims to identify something as 'unwanted' rather than the agency or intent in the act of perpetration (42). There is something unspoken about the quality of sexual harassment that lies in instinct and feelings, as one comedian put it:

> "So let's keep this simple, If it feels wrong it is wrong or if it feels creepy, it is creepy."
>
> (43)

To some extent, the harm caused is easier to define as we have more words available to use; what is making so many women feel creeped out, we do need to agree a handle.

WHAT SHALL WE CALL IT?

Academics have examined the history and meaning of 'acts of perpetration' (44) and there is no need to reproduce this work here (31,45). Labels do not tell us whose experience we are talking about or what that label misses out (46). In relation to sexual harassment, terms like, 'men's stranger intrusions' put the spotlight and agency firmly on the perpetrator (31). This book uses a range of terms that attempt to communicate some of the intent behind the behaviour such as 'sexual bullying'. However, the term is used interchangeably with sexual harassment/violence/abuse/assault throughout this book, connecting behaviours along the continuum of sexual violence (22). I refer to sexual violence as a single thing as well as a group of related acts using terms that reflect where I am coming from. The same is true of others working, writing, policing and prosecuting and as such, their words tell us about how they think about sexual harassment and bullying and abuse. No one needs to use my words but me.

In addition, should we tie the labels to the act or to the person and their identity? Should it be, 'acts of perpetration' (44) and 'experiences of sexual violence'? 'Victim/survivor' is commonly used to move someone who has experienced sexual violence beyond a victim identity but it is still a label for someone based on an experience they had (47). At the same time using 'perpetrator' frames sexual abuse/violence as something wrong with individual offenders; if the causes of sexual violence are much wider then this may simply not be good enough.

Whatever label is used, it should also encompass what is meant by it: in street sexual harassment, women are a sexualised object to comment on. If we begin to dig underneath the broad-brush prevalence statistics the fault lines of how such behaviour is targeted, it reveals an underlying story of gender and power. In case anyone doubted what and why, sexual bullying is there to police gender; it has meaning and intent.

CHAPTER 2

Hotspots – scope

GETTING FROM A TO B

> "At a train station exit, someone came behind me and touched my bottom. I looked around but because there were a lot of people milling around, I couldn't see who had done this to me. The rest of the time I spent waiting with my back to the wall in case it happened again."
>
> (29)

Ambiguous spaces provide an opportunity for people who perpetuate and make some forms of harassment harder for women to identify (48, 49). In a survey of women in London, 31% of women aged 18 to 24 had experienced unwanted sexual attention while on public transport in the previous year (50). Some go as far as to describe public transport as a 'crime attractor' for sexual offending (49).

Further research highlights the everyday nature of wolf whistles, groping and unwanted sexual comments experienced with international rates ranging from 15 to 95% (51). Women report more sexual harassment in places where behaviour is ambiguous or easily disguised as 'accidental' such as crowded public transport or night clubs (9). The British Transport Police say that busy carriages enable acts of perpetration to be masked as accidental sexual touching due to overcrowding or bumpy train travel (49). Targeting of women in isolated spaces, away from witnesses, also occurs in order to carry out public masturbation, exposure or sexual assault (52). Let us not forget the use of covert cameras for the purposes of image-based sexual abuse such as 'upskirting' (53) which has now become illegal (54).

The transitory nature of some situations especially on public transport, may mean women did not have time to recognise what was going on. This is compounded by the fleeting nature of incidents and no clear sense of who victim/survivors can appeal to for help. Transport for London describe this

DOI: 10.4324/9781003168591-3

as a 'perceived lack of capable guardianship' (49). Transport operators may be reluctant to overtly address sexual harassment, claiming the attention could make people feel unsafe. A reluctance that ignores that a large group using their services already feel unsafe and any lack of recognition of the reality may in fact communicate impunity to offenders (55). An increasingly documented problem is the open watching of pornography on public transport and the intimidating impact it can have on women around the perpetrator (56). The act itself communicates a male sense of entitlement and intimidation but also that public consumption of pornography is perfectly normal. Women also watch pornography and sometimes on the bus (57), but the issue of scale and scope situate it differently, it just does not mean the same thing. The characteristics of public transport that invite acts of sexual bullying can be seen in other spaces such as the night-time economy.

PART OF A NIGHT OUT

Sexual harassment through ambiguous physical contact is also found in the night-time economy in which female staff and clients report instances of sexual harassment being so commonplace that they are not even worth mentioning and certainly not worth reporting:

> "A lot will just think, oh I'm on a night out, that's fine, that's kind of what comes with it nowadays, which is really bad, really bad."
>
> (58)

Sexual harassment on a night out is reported by 63% women and 26% men, so much so that it has become 'part of the unwritten rules of a bar' (59). There is no clear messaging to contradict the assumption that if you want to go out you have to accept a certain level of uninvited touching and harassment. It seems unavoidable:

> "I was followed home by a man walking late into the night after a shift finished close by. I was very frightened, as he got closer, I turned around and bellowed FUCK OFF at him, spun around and ran off and managed to get home ok. The following night, I got a taxi home. Unfortunately, I sat in the front seat, where the taxi driver touched my leg and knee, and tried to grope me when we stopped for me to pay and exit the taxi."
>
> (60)

The responsibility to protect themselves is placed on women and requires simply not going to those places nor trying to get home safely from them. Men's role or contribution is somehow erased (61).

"I have avoided clubs entirely for a few years now as the harassment is not worth the night out for me."

(62)

What about alcohol and sexual harassment, surely it has an important role but is that as fuel for sexual violence, contributor to impaired judgement or is it a way to pick a vulnerable target? We know that drunk women are targeted more, victims are as much as twice as likely to report that they had had a drink (63). At the same time, in sexual assaults such as rape, double the number of offenders have been drinking (64). However, victims are also more likely to blame themselves if they have been drinking or using drugs (65); they are after all, part of a society in which women's behaviour is the focus of inquiry rather than men's offending (66). Victim/survivors have commonly been framed as somehow to blame for the attack, by being drunk or dressing attractively or being out at night, "you have to look at the way she was dressed, she was wearing a thong with a lace front" (67).

Other studies suggest that drinking plays a role in blurring boundaries for men (58,68) and potentially alcohol reduces women's ability to risk assess situations (65). It's use certainly increases the likelihood that the police will deem a rape case for 'NFA' or no further action (69). An innovative study that trained observers in bars to note harassment found that the men's aggressiveness did not match their level of intoxication, there was no relationship. Instead, men were seen to target women who were intoxicated (68). Therefore, alcohol may well play a role but more in who is attacked rather than who does the attacking.

Thinking about the places harassment happens in, we also need to look at how sexual bullying plays out in virtual spaces, especially as they have become central to our work and social lives through Covid-19 restrictions.

ONLINE

The evolution of social spaces encompasses rich online communities and we know that women in particular are heavily targeted for gender-based online abuse. Fifty per cent of young women aged 11–21 think that sexism is worse online than offline, with a further 23% having had threatening things said about them on social media, particularly when gaming (70,71). Sexual bullying includes public humiliation, on and offline, in relation to appearance, assumed sexual activity; sexualised name-calling and image-based sexual abuse (53). Women and girls are more likely to experience harassment online than men and boys (72) and are more vulnerable to grooming; being asked for personal details; receiving unwanted sexual comments; or receiving intrusive violent or offensive pornographic context (73).

Women who are seen to speak out such as journalists or politicians, come in for particular online bullying, to the level that one woman MP received 8,121 abusive texts between 1 January and 8 June 2017 (74); that is a rate of approximately 50 per day (75) and much of it is sexualised. Social media platforms such as Facebook and Twitter have become places where virtual violence and abuse against women is often perpetrated (76). The potential for abuse to extend beyond the constraints of location, time and identity seem to escalate the invasiveness of this type of gender-based sexual bullying. Anonymity may enable impunity and 59% of women experiencing online sexist or misogynistic abuse reported the perpetrator was a stranger (74).

This matters because online abuse can undermine women's voices and many are discouraged from taking public office or openly expressing opinions, stopping them taking part in democratic processes (77). Online communities may reflect wider society but the amount of abuse of women and girls seems amplified in this anonymous forum. The online world has been called a male created dystopia for women (74,76). In the Covid-19 driven mass migration to online working many organisations no longer felt the need to tackle workplace sexual harassment as people were not at work (78). However, research shows that understandably, online sexual harassment has increased, one in seven young women have experienced threats to share intimate images (image-based sexual abuse) (79), an experience that often overlaps with wider issues of intimate partner abuse (80).

At the same time, online spaces have also offered safe environments for people to share their stories of sexual abuse/violence in a way they had more control over such as the #MeToo hashtag, Reddit and Tumblr survivor boards and the Everyone's Invited website (7). Anonymous formal routes are increasingly being offered such as anonymous hotlines, prevalence surveys and Report and Support services (81).

Many forms of harassment go on in very public spaces, what is remarkable is that they go unchallenged, even when other people are present (82). For this we need to understand a bit about the bystander effect and how this can normalise sexual harassment but can also be a tool to intervene and therefore, an important means of stopping it.

BYSTANDER APATHY

The waiting room is slowly filling with smoke, no one reacts, you sit and wait for someone else to do something. This 'bystander' reaction or lack of it, has long been studied within psychology (83). When applied to sexual bullying, it is more damaging. Attacks taking place in full view of others, to which no one but the victim reacts, implies that whatever is happening is both not a problem and probably the victim's fault,

> "Don't we all inadvertently condone acts like these when we just sit quietly? I'm disgusted with those New Yorkers who witnessed a crime and just let it be."
>
> (84)

The harm of sexual harassment is often made worse by a lack of bystander intervention which is experienced as disorientating and isolating for victim/survivors, in effect 'gaslighting' them. It can feel like witness passivity endorses sexual harassment (85,86).

> "When I look back now, as an adult and a mother, I am horrified that none of the other adults around at the time intervened on my behalf as a child or reported the men to the council or the police."
>
> (87)

Women describe amplified feelings of shame when witnesses overtly ignore victimisation and how the inaction of others increases the harm (88). Only 20% of victim/survivors say someone else had responded to their need for help (89).

> "While you are going through the incident you still feel quite alone. If people don't have any reaction while someone is essentially violating your space then they . . . send the message that what that person is doing is acceptable on some level." Cisgender woman, heterosexual
>
> (89)

On the flip side, the opposite is also true in that the impact of harm can be reduced if bystanders do intervene and in so doing communicate to all that this behaviour is not okay, not the norm (89)

> "Another person intervened and said, 'Hey, that's not appropriate, what are you doing?' . . . It would feel more validated coming from a third party." Cisgender woman, heterosexual
>
> (23)

There has been a recognition of the key role of bystander training in addressing social norms on university campuses across the UK as well as in the US (82), but is there something about certain environments that makes sexual harassment more likely?

TOXIC ENVIRONMENTS

At the opposite end of the scale from virtual spaces are specific environments that emphasise gender power imbalances and may trigger territorial sexual bullying and harassment (90).

Where we work

#MeToo has left a wide range of employers scrambling to respond to allegations of sexual harassment (91). In a UK poll, 40% of women and 18% of men from a sample of over 6,200 people say they had experienced unwanted sexual behaviour in the workplace with 77% not reporting, mainly for fear of victimisation or feeling they cannot trust their employers (92,93). When asked simply if they were sexually harassed, people tend to report lower rates than if they are given a list of harassing behaviours. There is also a clear age difference in framing some of the milder forms of behaviour as harassment (20).

> "I am unsure if it would be classed as 'sexual' harassment but within the last two years I have had to file multiple complaints about a male co-worker who was stalking me, sending unwanted mail to my house and who cornered me in the car park at work."
>
> (94)

To reach the legal definition under the Equality Act 2010, the behaviour has to be:

- Unwanted conduct of a **sexual** nature
- Have the purpose or effect of violating a person's dignity (**intended or unintended**)
- Or of creating an intimidating, hostile, degrading, humiliating or offensive environment for them (**intended or unintended**) (37)

For obvious reasons, many serious forms of sexual harassment in the workplace happen in private yet many employers believe it is not a problem because they have not seen it happening (95).

Prevalence rates vary internationally, in the US, a 2016 report found rates of workplace sexual harassment between 25% and 85% amongst women (96). As the Women and Equalities report on workplace sexual harassment concluded (97), without robust prevalence and outcomes data we are in the dark about what happens or what helps. In the UK reports show rates of around 52% rising to 63% for younger women (97).

Different reporting rates could also be a side effect of the gender of those in charge. Female HR decision makers were almost twice as likely as men to say that sexism was a problem in their own workplace, 40% of female bosses versus 24% male bosses recognised it as an issue (97). In a poll of 150 MPs for the Young Women's Trust, whilst more than half of the female MPs had been personally aware of sexual harassment or abuse in Parliament, fewer than one in five male MPs said the same (98).

We can also link sexual harassment to other signs of inequality in the workplace such as the gender pay gap and the lack of diversity/women in senior positions (77). Patterns of sexual bullying, as in other contexts, follows a path of vulnerability mirroring identity-based discrimination on the basis of age, disability (99), sexuality (100), and race (101) as well as other circumstances that denote less power such as insecure contracts, illness etc. (102,103).

> "On reporting it to the other church leaders I was told to either shut up or leave my job. I was a single mum & needed the job so I put up with it for another 2 years."
>
> (94)

Formal routes or protections for reporting harassment, such as workplace tribunals, puts all the financial, resource and personal burden on the individual which the Equalities and Human Rights Commission have described as 'crushing'. Complainants need legal representation the cost of which is not covered in a successful award (95). HR disciplinary processes often lack transparency, timeliness or balance, can overuse inappropriate mediation approaches and be derailed and delayed by perpetrators taking leave (104). "Employers outgun the employee in terms of resource" (105) so women simply don't report. The Trades Union Congress (TUC) conclude it is "understandable that with the costs so high and the likelihood a good outcome so low, most sexual harassment in the workplace is rarely reported" (106).

Many women make informal 'adjustments' after experiencing sexual harassment such as avoiding the perpetrator through withdrawing from work relating to them, or simply leaving:

> "Reduced my hours at the university and only work in environments where I feel safe. I now never work alone with male students or members of staff as the situation is still difficult." Staff
>
> (107)

Most women just want it to stop and often it is easier to quit the organisation resulting in the systemic exclusion of women from career progression, male dominated key sectors and leadership roles (108). The impact of sexual harassment in the workplace undermines the contribution of women with obvious large economic knock-on effects (108). Failing to tackle sexual harassment at work is limiting women's contribution to a whole sector of society and allows covert sex discrimination to continue.

> "It took me filing a complaint against him with the police and a letter of concern to my HR manager for my employer to actually do something about his advances and prevent him speaking to me, and even then they changed my shift and disrupted my life, not his."
>
> (103)

There is also an element of shame-induced, learned behaviour with women both taking responsibility for and paying the cost of perpetrators sexual bullying.

> "On reflection I feel as if I sacrificed my integrity just so that these men didn't have to feel uncomfortable, because upsetting them was scarier to me." Staff
>
> (107)

When combined with the 'don't make a fuss' normalisation of sexual harassment, shame creates a pathway to silence around sexual violence and avoidant strategies ensure it continues (102).

Employers can be complicit in acts of avoidance. Non-Disclosure Agreements (NDAs) or 'gagging' clauses in employment or settlement contracts have been extensively abused to stop complainants speaking out about or reporting sexual harassment (109). A Select Committee Inquiry found they have been used to threaten, intimidate, bully and silence victims and are facilitated by the legal profession (97).

Often the perpetrators are senior, the victims junior and therefore the implications of complaining are stacked against the complainant, with organisations protecting seniority (95). Also telling is evidence from Business in the Community research which showed that senior female staff are targeted as a tool to reassert control where male power feels threatened (95); a way to 'put them back into their place' (110).

The Equality Act (2010) makes employers liable for acts of sexual harassment unless they have taken reasonable steps to prevent it (37). In the absence of a common code of conduct these steps translates into widely variable practice. Many, including public sector employers, do not have sexual harassment policies, do not collate data on sexual harassment or set out behaviour expectations in staff training (111). MPs have called this an 'epidemic' of inaction and poor practice, which remains unseen due to a lack of women in leadership roles (97).

Evidence also suggests that workplaces that do not tackle sexual harassment pay more than just settlement costs as the atmosphere created is not good for business, efficiency or teamwork, furthermore aggressive, hyper-masculine monocultures divide workers through excessive competition (108,112). Do we have to make the argument for diversity not just because it is right, not just because it can eliminate discrimination but because it makes good business sense and therefore money?

The unseen nature and gender blindness to the nuances of sexual bullying means that it is seen by most women as an 'occupational hazard' in working with men but is not openly addressed.

> "All the senior figures were male and he is popular with them nobody wants to be the individual making a fuss especially in a freelance

industry where you are employed not only on your skill but on your
likability."

(94)

A study of surgeons in Australia showed that authoritarian hierarchies and
'patronage-based' training systems, run by powerful senior (male) colleagues
drove sexual harassment (113). Such gender-based discrimination in workplaces mark out territory as 'reserved for heterosexual men' who police
this through sexual bullying within a harassment permissive environment
(93,114). Research is clear that men do experience sexual harassment as well
and may find it even harder to report (102).

Exaggerate any of the aspects described here or add in a concentration
of those groups that are more highly victimised such as younger women,
and the prevalence of sexual harassment may be so normal it becomes
wallpaper.

Where we study

Higher Education may well present the 'perfect storm' of factors that can
drive sexual harassment and other sexual violence (115), so much so that the
MPs looking at this area concluded; "sexual harassment and other violence
against women is blighting women's experiences of university" (116).

In 2010, of 2058 female students, one in seven reported experiencing a
serious physical/sexual assault at university and 68% had experienced verbal
or non-verbal abuse. Perpetrators were generally male students, known to
the victim/survivor, four in ten of whom then told no one (117).

Higher Education is full of young people who match the profile not
only for those likely to be victims (young women) but also more likely to
perpetrate (young men) (115). Hirsh and Khan's study describes US campuses as 'sexual assault machines' (44). Students are likely to socialise within
a new environment dominated by alcohol related events and taking place in
nightclubs, both of which we know contribute to the prevalence of sexual
harassment and violence (115). For some, it may well be the first time they
navigate sexual boundaries and safety with up to 36% starting university as
sexually inexperienced (Bristol Students Union, 2018). It is not a surprise
then to see that research points to a 'redzone' of sexual violence and abuse,
reported in the first few weeks of the academic year and often within freshers' events (118).

"Typical is a horrible way to put it, but as a second year, attending a
few freshers' events both years, I've seen a number of unwanted sexual
touching at freshers' events, I think it's very common because of the
way freshers and university is portrayed."

(119)

The role of group-based, male dominated societies has been linked to the dominance of 'lad culture' in higher education.

> "Lad culture seems to dominate some aspects of university life, notably certain social spheres (such as sports societies) many students tend to accept it as the way things are: it's normal; unremarkable."
>
> (120)

Unhealthy masculinity may be particularly potent where group norms have become concentrated such as sports teams or in the US college fraternities, where 'lad culture' often manifests through sexual aggression (121). A comprehensive study of US campuses (44) surfaced worrying power dynamics where only male fraternities can serve alcohol, therefore controlling the party scene.

Data about sexual violence on campuses is hard to assess. Universities in the UK have no legal obligation to collate or report data. In the US, a civil rights approach of protecting women's equal access to education dictates mandatory measurement and prevention of sexual violence under Title IX (115). This more standardised framework is called for in the Women's and Inequalities Committee report on sexual harassment (24) in place of the UK 'consumer protection' framing.

In the UK's now commercial Higher Education market, there are perverse incentives to ignore sexual harassment on campus in order to protect 'reputational risk' meaning that universities are fearful of becoming associated with the issue of sexual violence (115). Other trends have seen procedures attempting to emulate criminal justice processes with their inherent gap in providing justice (122). We have seen that sexual harassment and bullying is common throughout society. Some institutions have shown 'thought leadership' in this field by both openly acknowledging the problem and trying to count it and prevent it, including Durham University, Cambridge University and UCL, however, this is often reactive once a problem goes public (123).

Widespread but changing institutional passivity is grounded in previous guidance such as the 1994 Zellick report whose basic message to universities was to leave it to the police (124). Investigations into case studies of sexual harassment by university staff, 'Power in the Academy' evidenced a tendency for universities to treat incidents as one-offs with little reference or understanding of them as part of a wider culture of gender inequality (119). Progress has been made. Work by the Universities UK in 'Changing the Culture' (125) and groups like the 1752 group (126) have reformed guidance. The Office for Students (OfS) funded one-off 'catalyst' projects to increase reporting, promote bystander interventions and establish clear social norms campaigns (127) but tackling sexual violence remains optional and therefore variable. Even now, policies often do not require disclosure of personal relationships of staff with students (128). Instead, this is often left to the discretion of the staff member involved, based on their assessment of vague concepts such as 'conflict of interests', an approach which ignores the inherent power imbalance between staff and students (119). Good practice can be seen elsewhere such as Cornell University in the US, where an extensive community consultation drove changes in their policies around relationships based on more effective open conversation about how people should work together (129).

The setting of Higher Education is somewhere people study, live but also work. The environment is dominated by hierarchical systems where staff clearly have power over the student body (130). Steep power inequalities and hierarchical structures are particularly concentrated in the post-graduate and early career system that relies heavily on 'patronage' and where one report suggests four in ten students had experienced at least one sexualised behaviour from staff (119), a rate which may be worse for female post-graduates (131).

This reminds us that sexual harassment prevention in universities is often directed at students rather than staff. Evidence shows 'boundary blurring' behaviour by lecturers such as introducing the topic of sex as a 'matter for discussion' within one-to-one sessions or socialising with students is a red flag, especially if those lecturers are the gatekeepers of marks, references and future opportunities (119).

> "In all but two cases we encountered it has been heterosexual male lecturers seeking sexual relationships with female students younger than themselves; and that those who indulge in such behaviour once seem to do so repeatedly."
>
> (118)

US research has clearly mapped the lack of women across Science, Technology, Engineering and Medicine (STEM) (130) with greater sexual harassment problems reported in male dominated fields such as physics (132). The report linked rates to male dominated, hierarchical power structures centred around individuals. At the same time, they found tokenistic approaches to prevention and a lack of awareness or skills in senior management to tackle sexual harassment. This is how much of Higher Education works, some suggest it is integrally shaped by a culture of a specific kind of predatory heterosexual masculinity (133). Half of working women have experienced workplace sexual harassment (102) and some institutions have subverted the gendered burden into an issue of 'problematic women' rather than institutional failings in a reputational risk strategy (134). The intangible and ambiguous nature of sexual bullying has been used to frame women as unable to make sense of their own experiences, causing them to question their own judgement.

"I do now realise that this could potentially be defined as sexual harassment though and that I could/should have sought support earlier. I did mention it to a manager at the time but it did not go anywhere, mainly because I said it was not a big problem (which was not true looking back)."

(107)

Historically, there is also evidence that when sexual harassment is formally reported, those accused are simply allowed to resign with no formal disciplinary issues on their record, sometimes referred to as 'bouncing the perp', with instances of 'met with knowing smiles rather than strong disapproval' (135).

On the flip side, Higher Education may present a crucial timeframe or opportunity to intervene and address the social norms that incubate sexual offending (117). Student activists have proven to be a great resource that has driven much reform to date through protest movements such as Revolt Sexual Assault and the National Union of Students (117,136).

Framing campuses differently, as places of work for large academic and non-academic workforces, may allow greater use of workplace protections. The Women and Equalities Select Committee recommended employers adopt a code of conduct that requires much more rigorous application of 'duty of care' responsibilities. The Government Equalities Office has also been tasked with improving sexual harassment data (137). These policy changes are needed to evidence poor performance in addressing sexual harassment and violence (111,137). The Office for Students have more recently, issued a 'statement of expectations' (138) of what universities 'should' be doing to protect both students and staff.

The best form of evidence, based on a review of all the academic studies which are then assessed for their scientific strength (139), concludes that intervening in Higher Education is too late and that most efforts to change behaviour rely too heavily on one-off, short, college-based programmes such as bystander training. There is no clear evidence these work in actually reducing sexual violence (140). Schools should be the place to begin addressing the restrictive definitions of gender and sexual norms that connect directly to sexual harassment and sexual violence.

More recent school-based research by OFSTED, the school inspector, reports sexual harassment of girls at a level so high that many do not even think about reporting, with 92% seeing sexist name calling, sharing of explicit images and request for 'nudes' as normal (141).

University or education is a time when young people strive to find an identity and shape their goals as 'sexual citizens' (44). Let us not forget that students, who have by definition stayed in and can afford Higher Education, are different from other groups for whom 'place' may define where sexual bullying is more prevalent (142).

Power in short supply – place and poverty

Geography and place show different patterns of sexual bullying (90). We know that areas of deprivation have much higher rates of ill health (143), poorer sexual health (144) and more intimate partner violence (145,146). We also know that exposure to family violence may relate to later perpetration of sexual violence (147).

The common link behind these increased rates is how some men find identity. Performing masculinity is not fixed but fragile and told through repeatedly signalling it to others (148). Environments of strain and adversity through poverty or as people living in deprived areas of Glasgow called them, 'rough shit holes', can lay down a background of negative childhood experiences (149). Measures such as those of Adverse Childhood Experiences or ACEs, crudely score these and relate them to a range of negative outcomes (150,151). International research has consistently shown that this early adversity is powerfully tied to later perpetuation of sexual violence (152). Men, who as children, had been victims of physical or sexual violence, had experienced neglect, had witnessed violence against their mothers, were more likely to say they had committed sexual violence themselves. How does "I could hear my mother getting battered off the walls" (Ryan, 36 [150]) relate to acts of perpetration?

We will look at how lack of empathy towards women as well as sexual scripts that normalise sexual aggression, play a role in Chapter 6. Sexual abuse and violence may offer a short cut to being a 'real man' in places where opportunities to achieve status in positive ways (education, work) are limited. To 'be a man', with few ways of doing that and narrow definitions of what a real man is (the breadwinner; the car owner [153]) can result in 'protest masculinity' (148) or displays of 'hyper masculinity' through violence. This offers some men a way to overcome powerlessness as a reaction to poverty (148). Research carried out in very deprived areas in Scotland also found how men and women seemed to live separated lives, making seeing women as 'other' or 'objects' easier (149). Men in the study by Lorimer seemed completely lacking in empathy for women and blamed women for the sexual violence perpetrated against them. There was in these areas: "an undertone of simmering resentment towards women and some of the most aggressive views were reserved for those women who transgressed gender female norms of sexuality and sex" (149). This sexual aggression may be particularly used to police non-conforming women, again, as a way of putting them back in their place.

That may be why, for women living in poorer areas, there is a greater risk of sexual bullying (12) and intimate partner violence (145), to control: a dynamic some report openly recognising (146). Other research shows that working class women may be more at risk from sexual violence or rape as punishment (154). In order to understand sexual bullying, not only do we need to work out the causes, we need to see why it is worse in some places and not in others. Here we can begin to see what in public health is called a 'dose response'; less power means more sexual violence.

The irony is for men, any desire for intimacy and emotional connection is blocked by the need to be seen as self-reliant, manly and violent. That violence can equally turn inwards, connecting to higher rates of suicide (155).

How do young women experience this when moving around the places they live? They report experiencing sexual harassment and bullying from an early age (75) which then continues throughout their lives and the spaces they move through. The meaning of it seems easy enough to read: you are not safe, your appearance in public spaces attracts comment, is judged and is conditional on men's permission and approval.

> "Every time I walk out of the door, there is the potential of being made to feel like a piece of meat, waiting for a physical, verbal, and or psychological attack. It has often felt like I have to constantly evade and avoid unwanted contact. This is degrading and humiliating."
>
> (60)

That judgement is also conditional on how sexually available women appear and in the case of non-conforming groups, can make them a target of 'corrective' harassment to ensure they stick to the social norms of the female, attractive and up for it (100,156). As @Everyday Sexism's Laura Bates reminds us, this is not about biology, sex or something inherent and uncontrollable in men, this is deliberate, this is men choosing to assault and harass women (157). Sexual abuse geography (44) and the experience of street harassment communicates to women that you are in men's space.

In summary, we have seen that the hotspots of sexual bullying describe a structural pattern that maps onto social inequality. It is not about sex, it is about power. It happens throughout society but may be particularly an issue where female power encroaches on historical male privilege such as the workplace or where that male privilege is undermined by poverty. Sexual harassment/abuse crosses social spaces, it follows women from home, perpetuated by partners, through public places by strangers into work and education by colleagues and bosses. We will look at the role of the maps we use to make sense of it and how that changes our understanding in Chapter 6. For now, let us just log that where individuals experience sexual violence and who they tell, the families and communities in which it happens, the organisational responses that prevent or encourage it, is all wrapped up in the cultural framing of what it means. Such a wide view demands an 'ecological model', that captures the whole system, one that is already central to public health and its history of reducing harm and improving wellbeing through their broadest determinants (158,159). We see this not only in where it happens, but who it happens to.

CHAPTER 3

Who does it happen to?

Anybody can be a victim but not everybody is more likely to be victimised. It is not who they are but more about who they are not and what
they do not have: voice and/or power. Sexual harassment and abuse victimisation has meaning. That meaning varies by location, opportunity, who is
targeted and who is perpetrating but it still tells us the story of how easy it is
to victimise in order to show control. We only have to count the numbers
and look at the prevalence to see this.

WOMEN

Let us start with a clear message, the majority of victims experiencing or
reporting sexual offences are female. Statistics from 2018 show harassment,
abuse and violence mainly happens to women and girls (24). In the UK, 64%
of women have experienced sexual harassment in public places since they were
15 rising to 85% in younger women (160). This is not history, or something
that used to happened, 25% also said they suffered sexual harassment within
the last year. Few of those experiences translate into crime statistics, never-
theless approximately 560,000 females and 140,000 males reported being the
victim of a sexual offence (12). Within those figures, women were nearly four
times as likely as men to have experienced sexual assault although we do know
men report less (161). The types of women more often targeted are key.

THE YOUNG

It is important to recognise the ongoing burden of child sexual abuse and
how this connects to abuse later in life. From what we know (which is not
the whole picture), 1 in 20 children in the UK have been sexually abused
and girls are more likely to have experienced this (162). Data from the Office

DOI: 10.4324/9781003168591-4

for National Statistics show that females aged 10 to 14, 15 to 19 and 20 to 24 years were disproportionately more likely to be victims of sexual offences recorded by the police than any other age group. Similarly, males aged 5 to 9, 10 to 14 and 15 to 19 years were disproportionately more likely to be victims (12). The fact that child sexual abuse and sexual abuse of adults are reported separately should not allow us think that child sexual abuse is something different and separate. The young are particularly targeted as they have less power and that vulnerability is eroticised (163).

> "My 11 year old daughter was approached by a drunk man on her way home from school and was offered money for sex."
>
> (164)

Research found that most women surveyed said harassment began at a young age (9). More than one in four women said sexual harassment first happened to them before the age of 16, and more than three in four said it had happened by the age of 21 (165). Similarly, most women interviewed about their experiences said that they first experienced sexual harassment as a child/adolescent, often when walking home from school, often whilst in school uniform,

> "It's a really warped pervy old man thing." Lucy 19, Belfast
>
> (23)

Unsurprisingly, we see higher victimisation rates in schools and universities with greater prevalence than other settings (165).

As such, harassment begins at a formative age, it shapes the messages boys and girls get about what is acceptable behaviour between men and women (46). At the same time, girls are taught to minimise experiences of harassment and abuse; in effect, they are being trained to endure it (166). Public places become environments in which young women and girls 'appear or are looked at' but in which boys 'do or act' (167).

Work across 15 countries found common prevention messaging directed at girls framing them as both vulnerable to abuse and at fault for it, whilst boys were simultaneously framed as trouble (75). It is on entering public spaces that adolescent girls are first taught how they are to be seen and should therefore, see themselves. An influential report by the American Psychological Association (163), reviewed in 2019 (168), documents the consequences for girls in a range of negative impacts such as performance inhibition, self-objectification, eating disorders, low self-esteem and depression.

> "They felt that harassers exploited the perceived vulnerability of younger women, thinking they could 'get away with it' more easily as girls were less likely to 'fight back' or report."
>
> (169)

Compounding this experience is the widespread erasing of women and girls' reality; evidence shows girls are commonly told to ignore it and see sexual harassment as normal (170). Accepting abusive comments or wolf-whistles as part of your daily routine makes it even harder to draw a line of what is or is not acceptable. 'It was just a hand on the knee' (27) but is that hand an individual act, a compliment or part of a constant, cumulative 'training' that educates women and girls about their value, worth and who they can be in the world? That training is then mirrored in how we teach boys to become men (see Chapter 5).

VULNERABLE GROUPS

Other groups targeted are people with disabilities, especially women, who are more likely to report having experienced non-volitional sex (171) and workplace sexual harassment (99). People with disabilities (172) and those with special educational needs (173) are at particular risk of a range of abuse and report the highest levels of both severe and physical bullying in schools, as are children with mental health problems (174). Vulnerability and mental health are difficult to disentangle into clear cause and effect; child sexual abuse does impact adult mental health (175) and is clearly linked to a range of early childhood experiences that tie in with both victimisation as a child and adult mental health problems (176).

> "I also have PTSD from childhood sexual abuse and abusive high school relationships, so when street harassment occurs, it worsens my existing PTSD."
>
> (177)

Vulnerability may be read as ease of victimisation but also, for perpetrators, a means of avoiding sanction; Chapter 6 looks at those less believed within the criminal justice system. Vulnerability also overlaps with 'difference' or 'otherness' again demonstrating the 'hate crime' role of sexual harassment as marking territory and signalling power (178). Ease, lack of credibility and difference attract abuse but also speak to why groups are targeted.

RACE AND INTERSECTIONALITY

We have seen how just being a woman or being young or having a disability increases the chance you will be sexually abused. Racially minoritised women and girls are even more likely to be victims of sexual abuse (179). A pattern of abuse that is consistently focused on a profile of different characteristics is an expression of systematic inequality and speaks to the function of control through that harassment (180).

"We cannot 'leave race out of it' because the way we are treated is based on how our whole identities are perceived as black women. This harassment and abuse often uses racist stereotypes and insults as an attempt to put black women in our place."

(181)

Despite sexual abuse and violence against marginalised women being greater, it is less researched. 'Where are the Black girls in our services, studies and statistics?' is a report that highlights a gap around child sexual abuse (182). In the UK, there have generally only been small numbers of local studies (183). Work in the US shows the same mismatch between scale of racial victimisation and the lack of research on it (184–186); is this a systematic looking away?

Washington's 20-year-old study (184) with US rape advocates gave us a glimpse into what shapes who and when racially minoritised women tell, presenting a complex picture of internal, familial and cultural factors. Some barriers come from within women's own communities (187), especially where cultural and familial stigma exaggerates existing shame around sexual abuse (188). Other victim/survivors speak of being stuck in the strong Black women stereotype; as Sophie describes, "Black women are raised to be superwomen" (184).

Not only do Black victims of sexual abuse have to 'act strong' but sexualisation of their bodies (189) and identities underpin racist responses; "my experiences are different as a black woman. I should be 'up for it' or 'I am fair game'" (181). Work by Michelle Jacobs in the US describes a trio of ways racially minoritised women's experiences of sexual and domestic violence are discredited: she is portrayed as promiscuous, her word is worth less and she is more aggressive or likely to use violence (190). This racism may come from historical, colonial sources but figures in women's everyday experience of criminal justice and support agencies (186,191).

We see a further concentration of factors in insecure migrant status which encompasses linguistic and legal barriers and a lack of knowledge of support agencies (192). If they cannot speak the language and do not know who to contact, how do victim/survivors get help, especially if they are excluded from support services; migrant women in the UK have 'No Recourse to Public Funds' (193). Asylum seekers have seen their sexual abuse 'story' negated as being a ploy to gain refugee status (183). The Refugee Council's review of literature points to the role of migration in increasing male perpetration; loss of status through migration and changed gender roles can drive increased intimate partner/sexual violence (194).

There seems to a tipping point where the harm overtakes the need to stay silent and the need to tell overwhelms avoidant coping mechanisms, a point when women do reach out (183). It is at this point, work by Maier in the US clearly tells us, that African American women were more likely to see medical and criminal justice agencies as the primary sources of re-victimisation (185). Racially minoritised groups may avoid police reporting within the context of lived experience of repeated long-term racially profiled policing; one woman described it like this:

> "I never felt that the police were someone to turn to because I see too much of their abuse in communities that I have lived in." Scorpio
>
> (184)

Although FGM (female genital mutilation), forced marriage and honour killings register on a continuum of cultural oppression (183) agencies can fail to see beyond them to recognise general sexual abuse. It is not really a surprise then that existing services are seen as inaccessible and under- utilised by racially minoritised women (195).

This includes rape support services in which there may be a lack of diversity (196); women need to see themselves in the help they are offered, to know that the complex picture of their experience out there will be understood,

> "There are so many other layers and personally as a black woman, I feel like there are disadvantages that they will luckily never experience. I feel like if I was sitting opposite a woman who could identify and was not white-washing what I was saying we could get to the root causes a lot quicker."
>
> (183)

Beyond lack of diversity, research attests to a need to recognise that black women may also be required to adhere to a 'black cultural mandate to protect male offenders' (184). Access to and handing out of justice around sexual offences is different, fractured by racism, and the criminal justice response to sexual abuse and violence is examined in Chapter 6, but male dominance permeates the full range of support agencies. One Black woman's experience of white medical professionals led her to conclude:

> "Given those kinds of experiences with a medical authority, why would I seek out medical attention in a situation as crazy-making as rape." Carrie
>
> (184)

More research needs to be undertaken in racially minoritised communities to uncover the scale and nuance of the issue (185). However, layers of shame from friends, family and community agencies are amplified in the intersectional and cultural experiences of some groups. Some cultural contexts emphasise female purity and virtue, silence around sexual abuse is seen as essential, victims have been schooled in denial and self-blame (183). We can begin to understand how the tools of silence, such as shame and blame, deepened through racism, stop women getting help (197).

If sexual violence is 'crazy making', why would you make it worse by telling and inviting agencies that take away your control or undermine your story. Sexual bullying communicates something about who should be safe and who does not have the right. These boundaries of power can also be used to mark those who do not fit stereotypes or choose to step outside them.

NON-CONFORMING GROUPS – WHO YOU SHOULD BE

Studies show that awareness of difference or non-conformity starts young and both boys and girls pick up on gender non-conformity (75). This attracts significant pressure to conform to what is seen as gender-appropriate behaviours, an intolerance found to be greater amongst boys (75) in an effort to try and to police the 'man box' (198).

Prevalence of sexual bullying also focuses on gender non-conformity, a survey by the TUC found that seven out of ten (68%) of 1,001 LGBT respondents had experienced at least one form of sexual harassment at work and LGBT women experienced significantly higher levels of sexual harassment and sexual assault in a range of forms, including unwelcome sexual messages, sexual advances and sexual assault (100).

As one woman describes, simply the appearance of gender non-conformity attracts bullying.

> "During my late teens [date] and onwards, I found large and small groups of men aged 20s–30s would aggressively approach me while passing me on the street in [location] city centre while walking alone. They would demand to know if I was a man or woman, whilst surrounding me, or standing in my way . . . I yelled 'I am a woman'. I felt frightened, intimidated and shamed. If they were especially persistent I would have to pull my clothes so that it was obvious that my body parts were female. This happened as often as two or three times a week for approximately five years. . . . This has contributed to feelings of intimidation, fear of walking about, and shame about how I look. This still impacts my life contributing to anxiety."

(60)

A 35- to 44-year-old lesbian woman recalls,

> "I was told that all I needed was a good dick inside me and I'd be straight and also what a waste it was for all men that I was a lesbian."

(100)

Focusing sexual abuse on non-conformity represents a toxic combination of misogyny and homophobia (156) and says everything about how to be a man through the social policing of women, especially those who are 'incorrectly female'.

> "I think women who are gay or less feminine appearing have a
> more horrendous time in general . . . people who are threatened with
> rape because they look 'butch' or not feminine."
>
> (169)

Sexual bullying as punishing difference connects us to sexual violence in its historic and geo-political context and wider use in conflict: rape as an act of war is about dominance not sex or gender (199).

MEN AS SURVIVORS

Men can be victims and women can be perpetrators, the evidence that women and girls are more likely to experience sexual harassment/abuse on a greater scale and across a wider scope does not dismiss the harm also perpetrated against men and boys.

Crime statistics reported in 2018 show the majority of those reporting sexual assaults were female (approximately 560,000) but 140,000 were male (12), rising to 619,000 females and 155,000 males in 2020 (200).

Most victim/survivors of all genders do not disclose and society's construction of masculinity (see Chapter 5) means that disclosure may be particularly hard for men (201). Male on male rape was not illegal until 1994 and men share the impact of a society educated on victim blaming rape myths such as 'men cannot be raped' (202). As Elton Jackson from Survivors UK (the largest support charity for male victim/survivors) states, men may not tell anyone they have been raped because it can "shatter their masculinity" (203) the impact of which can be devastating:

> "It all hit me and I started to think 'I don't want to live with this, I don't
> know what to do'. If it wasn't for the thought of the devastation for
> my family and friends, I would have jumped off that bridge." Sam,
> 22-year-old male survivor
>
> (204)

Sexual violence against men and boys is widely underreported (156) and survivors are kept silent by the social norms that do not even recognise their trauma (161).

Where these experiences may be different is in the scope of what that sexual violence means for women and girls, and the all encompassing nature of everyday experiences of sexual harassment in the street, in educational institutions, at work and at home. Even getting home from a night out can result in kidnap, rape and murder and the fear of this becoming their story permeates women and girls navigation of the world.

The role of Public Health is to reduce harm and requires we prioritise work on women and girls because of the scope and scale of their victimisation. Most sexual bullying is committed by young men against women and 90% of those men will be 'known' to the victim/survivor (205). This should not eclipse male suffering which should also be addressed, not instead of but alongside working with women and girls. Multiple identities of gender, race and sexuality do not add to a victimisation score but pushes us to understand what sexual violence and abuse is for and who it benefits, something we can read from who it harms.

The common thread is the scope of male violent social norms against women and girls; boys and men; and against themselves (206).

CHAPTER 4

What is the harm?

HARM, A PUBLIC HEALTH PERSPECTIVE

> "It's been almost 30 years since I was abused, but I still have night-
> mares. 30 years later and the person who hurt me still haunts me.
> I woke up screaming last night just at the thought of being in the same
> room as him. I can't forget. I can't forgive."
>
> (#MeToo 2021)

What is the impact on the mainly women and girls but also men and boys, who have gone through sexual trauma? The harms include, superficially, the risk of physical injury (207,208) sexually transmitted disease, pregnancy, sexual or gynaecological problems (209) and somatic complaints such as pelvic pain (210). These more obvious, physical consequences also extend to a reduction in 'triggering' attendance at cervical smear screening, leading to greater risk of undetected cancer in survivors (211).

The less visible and often more enduring psychological costs are also high with almost all female sexual assault survivors experiencing significant post-traumatic symptoms in the immediate aftermath of an assault (212). The ripple effect or legacy of that emotional trauma throughout the life course is shocking. Around half the survivors continue to experience these symptoms three months later (213). A review of all the published evidence showed that sexual assault had a uniquely toxic effect and was closely linked to a range of long-term mental health problems (214) such as suicide, depression, anxiety and the knock on, self-treatment or coping manifestations of this pain in eating disorders, drug and alcohol dependence (215).

The harms endured are ongoing; a large, international study found that amongst 68,894 people across 26 European countries those who had been raped were nearly five times more likely to meet the diagnostic criteria for PTSD (Post Traumatic Stress Disorder) than those experiencing other forms of

DOI: 10.4324/9781003168591-5

trauma (216) with characteristic thought intrusions, sleep disturbance, generalised sense of unsafety and hypervigilance (217). Handling that can be like trying to ignore a car alarm going off in your head (218). The most common impact found in research by the National Union of Students was anxiety, followed by depression (219). A survey of current patients diagnosed with severe mental illness found 61% of female patients reported experiencing sexual violence as an adult (40% rape or attempted rape), 10% within the last year (220).

> "The threat responses that creep in and can really last for years, you
> can not realise that it is all connected to trauma." Micheala Coel
>
> (221)

Perhaps obviously, sexual abuse/violence combined within Intimate Partner Violence (IPV) can be even more toxic, where sexual bullying is part of a wider pattern of abuse over time (222). Even beyond physical and psychological impacts, sexual assault in your past predicts sexual assault in your future and those that have experienced sexual abuse before 17 years of age are more likely to be re-victimised (223).

One way in which the harm of sexual abuse trauma may be translated into longer-term problems is through insomnia, a well-recognised feature of PTSD (210,224). Sleeplessness can contribute to other mental health issues but might also act as a bridge to later physical ill health (225). Problems with sleeping within sexual abuse survivors is higher (226) and sleep as the ultimate vulnerability is by its nature, built on a feeling of safety (225). Not only do those experiencing sexual violence and abuse feel belittled, humiliated, objectified and violated but often exhausted (224).

The impact of sexual abuse/violence is a worldwide problem the consequences of which represent a significant and widely acknowledged public health burden (227,228). This is not happening in a vacuum but as part of a wider context, allowing, permitting and promoting sexual bullying across and throughout women's lives.

CUMULATIVE EFFECT

> "My first memory of street harassment was at the age [15–18] when
> I was out walking with my boyfriend during the daytime and a group
> of men stood outside a pub, drinking shouted 'you fucking slag!' at
> me. I was terrified and upset. . . . Since then, I have been subjected to
> hundreds of examples of unwanted attention in the streets."
>
> (229)

Statistics, criminal justice and formal reporting mechanisms often result in the depiction of sexual violence as an incident rather than locating it in the

WHAT IS THE HARM?   33

pattern experienced by women on a day-to-day basis (46). Not all women experience serious sexual assault, but most have stories to tell of sexual harassment when taking a bus, walking down the street, doing their jobs or studying (24).

> "When you get to the point where it is happening two/three times a
> week, at 9 o'clock in the morning, it makes me feel powerless."
>
> (230)

Testimony to the Women and Equalities inquiry on sexual harassment in public spaces (24) highlighted that young victims often do not understand what is happening and feel they have contributed to their own victimisation. One young witness had previously never told anyone about being touched and masturbated at in public (24). The repeated feelings of shame and fear, the drip feed of confusion and disorientation, works to prevent women and the bystanders around them reporting and combating harassment (86).

The mental energy required to pay attention to how women interact with the world in a way to minimise sexual harassment has been called 'safety work' (231). The feeling of constant threat and the need to be ever vigilant for risk or to manage your responses, takes up space and energy.

> "Ignoring men makes them angry and volatile. Politely saying no invites
> them to try harder to 'get me'. Responding aggressively puts me at
> risk of physical harm too. There is literally no way to stop harassment
> happening on our own."
>
> (229)

Walls of silence and blame surround such experiences in a society in which about one-third of people believe women who flirt are partially responsible for being raped (232) and amplifies the harm (see Chapter 6). What is different for women is the blanket nature of constant harassment that "in a small way builds up and wears you down" and "makes you feel under siege" (233).

Sexual bullying is a burden both at the time but also in its sum effect, it reminds women of the threat of something worse (22) and with that, the need to change the way you live to avoid it.

IMPACT – ERASE YOURSELF

Young victims talk about how parents have tried to protect them by restricting their freedom, "now my parents are more cautious . . . which affects my plans and my work if they can't always pick me up" Malikah 19, Birmingham (85).

Older women facing harassment also report continued use of withdrawal as a coping mechanism demonstrating a lifetime of minimisation:

> "It was the violence of his comments, the sexual references words like 'anal rape' and other revolting things he said, I also felt powerless to do anything. . . . I also thought that if I felt like that as a ([45–54] yr old woman who can handle herself) how would a 16 yr old girl feel if it happened to her. . . . But it has put me off going out and being in vulnerable situations or made me be more aware of potential risks in seemingly 'safe' high street places."
>
> (234)

Studies show women change or edit their lives, on a daily basis, to accommodate the range of sexual micro-aggressions and the threat of more serious sexual bullying through invisible acts of self-protection or 'safety work' (169,231) which may not be successful:

> "Some guy was talking about my arse and my tits and I turned round and told him to fuck off and he kicked my shopping out of my hand, into my road, sprayed it everywhere."
>
> (230)

The need to minimise yourself or 'become less', represents a systemic reduction in the freedoms and civil rights of women (77). The fact that witnesses rarely intervene underlines the message for women that it does not matter, which can be disorientating, isolating and is experienced as endorsement (85).

> "If you normalise and accept street harassment then you're starting to say it's OK for the next thing to happen, and it's an escalating process. It's a basic human right to be able to walk around and just live your life. No one is taking it seriously." Lindsay
>
> (85)

Access to public space, work and study are basic rights but experiences of sexual harassment transform access into something that is 'granted' to women by men and that comes at the price of feeling or being unsafe. Women therefore self-limit (what to wear, how much to drink, where to walk) and are forced to see their own bodies or sexual agency as a source of shame (160). The inevitable lesson girls and women learn in this gendered socialisation is that it is a man's world (235).

WHAT DOES RECOVERY LOOK LIKE?

One way of understanding the impact of sexual abuse and violence is to look at what survivors need to recover. There is a growing understanding of the importance of sexual abuse survivors being able to tell, take control of their own story and be heard (236).

Guidance on hearing initial disclosure focuses on the need to take a trauma informed approach and the mindful use of language to interrupt patterns of shame and blame (237). Response models such as BLOG (Believe, Listen, Offer – options, Get support for yourself) (123) or SEEK (Safety, Empower, Empathise and Know your role models) (238) include common elements of active listening, believing and providing the victim/survivor with options to restore control over what happens. The emphasis is on giving back something that defines what sexual violence and abuse is for, control.

Sexual harassment and bullying bring a particularly toxic silence, the additional harm of which may block the sense-making and retelling that build recovery. Labelling and disclosing are often the first steps to recovery either through access to specialist help or simply processing through retelling. Recovery from trauma requires *"being truly heard and seen by the people around us, feeling that we are held in someone else's mind and heart"* (239).

> "You can't really heal, if you can't talk about what you need to talk about, you can't heal properly." Anna, survivor
>
> (240)

Being heard is one of a variety of survivors' needs which one study described as a kaleidoscope (241). 'Justice' for survivors was found to include the need for dignity, voice, community, reclaiming identity and rejection of victim identity or what sexual assault says about the victim. These elements represent what they have lost and what harm has been caused. Other work speaks of agency, recognition, empowerment (242) and studies with people who have experienced child sexual abuse found a need for self-efficacy, self-confidence and self-worth (243) often attained through activism or advocacy work on behalf of others.

Through what needs to be regained, power, a voice and connection, we can see the impact on survivors but also the stark contrast with what the available criminal justice options offer. Many have to learn to live with the injustice and with the anger that feeds.

> "Justice, I'd like to say it's in my head, it's how I feel about justice, because I'll never get the justice that I want, because he was found not guilty in court."
>
> (240)

Perhaps framing survivors' pathway as one of 'recovery' rather than 'justice' offers more choice. Existing reporting options all seem to pivot around the search for criminal justice that can often lead to further legal dis-empowerment (244). The evidence base shows a mixture of experiences but many found it re-traumatisation (245). Telling in environments that contest the truth of their experience may not support recovery for survivors (246). My own research around sexual abuse/violence groups and how participants experience improvement often found a need to hold injustice and anger for failed criminal justice proceedings and focus on wider recovery or moving forward in other ways (240). Whilst #MeToo declarations shone a light on a less costly way for survivors to give testimony in an environment that felt safe (247), what is our wider societal obligation to listen? The responsibility of the listeners is to hear, understand and address the changes needed for prevention. For this reason, we need to better surface the role and function of sexual harassment and abuse.

CHAPTER 5

What is it for?

M ost men do not sexually harass or assault, however, almost all women (in certain age groups [9]) are sexually harassed by men (248), so who is carrying out these acts of perpetration? Research around this topic is most developed in Higher Education settings: useful, but not a representation of wider society (142). We know that convictions for rape are at the lowest level on record (249) therefore criminal offending rates are unlikely to give an accurate picture of perpetrators. International prevalence research shows that in various populations, up to 24% of men report perpetrating acts of sexual violence by their fourth year at university (250) (US). The international evidence speaks of key similarities across the world with between 26.8% (in Chile) and 51% (US) reporting having sexually harassed since the age of 14 (251) and how these acts of perpetration mean the same thing (152).

Yet, media coverage of sexual abuse/violence tends to erase the role of the perpetrator focusing on victim or location (252) and on rape myth informed narratives of stranger rape (253): despite 90% of victims knowing the perpetrator (205). Coverage uses passive language (254) around perpetrator agency or frames sexual abuse or violence as nothing more than a 'one-off' by a 'monster' (255), but why not make the connections to how we chose to organise our worlds around strict stereotypes of gender? In the UK, a man kills a woman on average every three days, that man is generally her current or former partner (26), intimate partner violence/domestic violence and sexual violence appear separate in the research and intervention literature but they are part and parcel of the same continuum and have the same role. We label these crimes in the passive voice as Violence Against Women and Girls. Why can't we talk about who did it and why?

DOI: 10.4324/9781003168591-6

ROUTES TO ACTS OF PERPETRATION

Research picks out a variety of reasons why people commit sexual violence/ abuse; these can be as a result of biological, developmental, cultural, social and mental health problems (256). This is a brief overview from a non-expert perspective, greater complexity, depth and knowledge can be found elsewhere (257). The core message from this literature is that you need to look at the individual to understand their motivation and that there is not a 'one size fits all' answer to sexual offending.

Multinational research (152,258,259) ties the likelihood of acts of perpetration to a range of factors that include:-

- Early childhood experiences of adversity, measured by ACEs or Adverse Childhood Events
- Witnessing domestic violence at home
- Hostile masculinity that endorses rigid gender roles
- Impersonal framing of sex
- Excusing of sexual aggression
- Internalised stigma
- Acculturation
- Alcohol use
- All-male social networks
- Approval of sexual aggression or 'rape myth' acceptance

A review of all the research found that concepts of what it means to 'be a man' expressed as 'hostile' or 'hyper-masculinity' have the largest predictive power of subsequent sexual violence (260). These studies suggest that the desire to control or dominate women and a defensive and distrustful orientation towards women are fundamental drivers. What is the pathway between the two? It is not uncommon for previous neglect and abuse to produce unbearable feelings of weakness and vulnerability (261) that individuals try to resolve through brutalising or dominating others in an effort to reclaim self-esteem (262). Add to this the contributory role of pornography as both 'bad sex educator' (263) and fuel for expression of existing gender hostility (Chapter 6) and we begin to see a plausible line of causality, however, we need more evidence from the lived experience of boys and men (264).

Combining the two elements of being exposed to aggressive pornography and experiences that harm the development of empathy, could enable sexual violence in providing both the plot (sexual abuse as way to reclaim threatened masculinity is normal) and the script (this is how you objectify women [265]). Acts of perpetration may require you to believe a narrative that women want to submit and resistance should be overcome (265). Where does this plot come from? Porn content reproduce this plot again and again (266) and it echoes through the rest of society, replicating common rape myths in the media (267) and informing rape trial juries (268).

> "We also found compelling evidence that too many boys believe that they have an absolute entitlement to sex at any time, in any place, in any way and with whomever they wish. Equally worryingly, we heard that too often girls feel they have no alternative but to submit to boys' demands, regardless of their own wishes."
>
> (1)

Men who admit to rape have more sexual partners, more transactional sex and commit more intimate partner violence or violence outside the home (269), a behaviour that often begins when they are young (152).

What are the connections that the research evidence demands we make to wider social attitudes and inequality (270)? The complexity of reading across individual experience and choices, the role of friends and family, community and society can be hard to conceptualise. You can frame people who perpetrate as supported by layers of a pyramid. These include 'facilitators' or 'cultural standard bearers' who affirm or do not call out the behaviour whilst others champion gender hostile beliefs, normalising sexual aggression (248). Further interaction between levels have been well described in comprehensive models (114) but most important is the recognition that sexual bullying is founded on social inequality expressed in individual behaviour; "Rape is no more about sex than hitting someone with a frying pan is about cooking" (248).

The ultimate trigger for sexual aggression may be female rejection of a male, threatening their manhood (271). Rejection is a short-cut to shame, something that undermines male entitlement to attention, the time of day, a smile, sex or staying in a relationship (272).

> "If you ignore, answer back or politely reject the man's comments you can be subjected to a torrent of vile abuse."
>
> (164)

Interpersonal threats to male power are easier to identify within examples of workplace sexual harassment where women's intrusion into male roles and status attract increased sexualised, social policing (273). We can see it elsewhere (public spaces, education) but the function is the same, to defend and maintain male dominance (patriarchy) (206,270). Our society's collusion in gaslighting victims through rape myths, allowing intrusive flirting to be declared 'flattery' (274) and criminal justice failings (Chapter 6), invalidates victims feelings of violation but also ensures their powerlessness is made clear.

Sexual bullying or abuse is not only one way back from shame or perceived weakness but evidences the sense that taking and having sex is part of one's identity 'as a man' (260). In identity theory, setting out who you are by what you do helps organise or make sense of your life (275) but contradictions to that picture are experienced as a threat (276). The maintenance of 'a real man' identity requires it to be consistent, to differentiate you from non-conforming others and give you a sense of confidence/control and self-esteem (277) or belonging or purpose (275).

At an individual level, some men may use sexual bullying to save themselves from shame, the research supports the theory that those who perpetrate are not made but taught this behaviour and are grown in environments of powerlessness (270). The 'men are made to seek out sex' ideas in biological or evolutionary theories of sexual aggression that underpin evolutionary psychological rationales for sexual abuse/violence, or 'evo-psychos' (278) are easily dismantled (279).

Even within flawed crime statistics on offending, we find patterns that show the highest rates of sexual abuse and violence perpetration among young, adolescent men (12). At the same time, young men are also more likely to stop (280,281), with the lowest recidivism rates post psychoeducational and Cognitive Behaviour Therapy-based interventions (280). In a review of all studies (258), desistence or stopping is associated with reduced hostility to women and more rejection of allied rape supportive beliefs; and a reduced sense that peers approve of forced sex or of the need to have lots of sex and partners (282). Therefore, problematic attitudes and behaviours can be unlearnt, an important test within public health is proving that reducing the cause then reduces the harm.

There is no one cause or one solution. Recognising motives behind perpetration does not make anyone less accountable for their choices. Perpetration for some may be strongly influenced by life history while for others, social norms and prejudices affirmed through peer approval, poor sex education and toxic environments are more influential. Those using sexual bullying may range from the confused and ill-informed to the driven and focused (257). When looking at the role of prevention, we need to ask the right questions, what is our society teaching young people about how to be a man and how to have sex and can we screen for greater vulnerability?

That understanding must go further and be set against a comprehensive model of factors and how they interact (114). We can see how society/cultural level issues such as masculinity, male dominance, devaluing women and legal impunity are echoed at a smaller scale in failed sanctions, norms of entitlement, honour codes, sex discrimination, gender stereotypes and hate groups (283). All of this can be amplified in pockets of poverty through social exclusion and depleted resources. Ultimately, these factors filter through to family stress, family gender stereotypes and obedience requirements, lack of individual opportunities, early trauma, poor parenting and hostile masculinity/norms of depersonalised sex (114). This multi-level map of factors might feel too complex but at its heart is how to get and keep power.

Understanding what behaviour is expressing allows us to see how it can be changed. We have seen that narratives of male dominance show the path for sexual aggression and drive the need to follow it, for some more than others. In Chapter 2 we looked at how place and poverty feed low status and therefore greater use of problematic forms of masculinity. Sexual violence is power and sexual victimisation is powerlessness. We need to look more closely at the way men (and women) are constructed.

MAKING MEN

> "It is alarming that one of the reasons they believed their behaviour to be acceptable is that they have seen other men behave in such a way. Unless and until boys are taught that the behaviour they see from older men is not acceptable and that it must not be copied, I cannot see how the cycle of harassment will end."
>
> (87)

What makes men 'real men'? Aggressive assertion of heterosexuality through sexual verbal or physical bullying seems to be part of that (284). Understanding variation in populations allows us to confirm the relationship theory via a 'dose response' (more of one leads to more of the other). Where other routes to manhood are closed down, such as in areas of high poverty, sexual violence may be a status short cut (285). This type of masculinity needs to be 'performed' to male friends (8,286) who heavily police it to make sure it is done properly (287). Young men live in fear of failing to live up to contemporary gender norms (288).

> "Guys aren't doing it because they want to date you, they're doing it to demonstrate their manhood." Lindsay
>
> (85)

'Man points' are earnt from proving objectification of women to their peers through sexting and sharing pornography (30) and it functions as a form of male bonding (160).

> "It's a performance. So, if a male does it, it's a performance of what he thinks it is to be male they're not really even doing it to speak to the girl. . . . They're just doing it as a laugh between themselves."
>
> (8)

Understanding the central ingredient of group display (286) in sexual bullying within problematic forms of masculinity helps contextualise the widespread nature of sexual harassment in public places (24). One problem with this type of masculinity is that its attainment is based on fictional ideals of an action hero, an ironically fragile form of male identity that therefore requires repetition (289). Promundo, an organisation working to promote gender equality by engaging men and boys, group the requirements of masculinity around a constellation of characteristics and describe it as a 'man box' (152,198). A 'real man would never say no to sex' or 'guys should act strong even when they feel scared'. These same men are ten times more likely to have harassed. Promundo describe how the limits of who boys and men can be are dictated by a need to appear self-sufficient and tough, coupled with physical attractiveness and always being up for sex: intimacy without any of the emotional range of being intimate (198). You must act tough and enforce rigid gender roles by being overtly heterosexual and absolutely not gay, using aggression to enforce control (198).

We have examined the negative consequences of sexual violence and abuse for women in terms of violence and sexual aggression but it is worth recognising the double-edged sword as the 'man box' harms the men that seek to live within its limits (290). International studies show the consequences of male violence on poor mental health, depression and suicide (155). Success at establishing a male identity can lay the foundations of emotional and physical ill health (290) as males become isolated, removed from others and cut off from both nurturing and support, truly the last action hero (289). Dismantling key elements of the man box can reduce sexual aggression (282) and work to engage men and boys seeks to give them permission to reclaim access to the full range of their own emotions and the expression of these through caring, vulnerability and alternative roles such as nurturing fatherhood (291), allowing men different ways of being a boy or man.

Widespread sexual abuse and violence is unlikely to happen without social support and a wider goal. We can also recognise similar patterns of behaviour in the parallel field of social inequality. Intersectionality between gender and racial inequality goes beyond their similar expression. Racism exists because it benefits members of the dominant race (292), it does a job. In sexual violence cases, white suspects are significantly more likely to avoid further investigation, especially if the victim is from a minoritised group, whilst offenders are more likely to be prosecuted if they are from a minoritised group (69). In the same way, sexual bullying in all its forms, is the expression of unequal power between men and women and a crucial social mechanism to maintain one group's subordination (293).

Can #MeToo make a difference? Possibly, but the conversations needed should not only be led by women. One survey of men aged 18–55 found just under half had not discussed #MeToo with anyone (294). Despite this, there has been a shift in what many men see as acceptable behaviour (295) which is ongoing that as cases continue to emerge (296). Legal or policing reform are often the focus for redress but parliamentary inquires do not find a lack of laws but an issue of enforcement (137). Access to and the resources within these systems are still dominated by narratives around false claims, victim blaming and rape myths and are examined more in Chapter 6.

Sexual bullying, sexual abuse and violence are ways of enacting male dominance as well as regulating oppressed groups or hoarding status (284). This is unlikely to be experienced as a conscious act but more the manifestation a belief in a sense of entitlement: 'what I want comes first'. The harassment method of boundary marking of non-conformity takes other forms such as homophobia (100). So, to answer the question, what is sexual violence for: it is for the male social policing of territories of power and authority; it is to underline women's conditional rights to resources such as public or online spaces, education or work; and to signal male priority access to sex as a proxy for access to society's resources.

Systems – criminal justice, policing, protection of human rights and most importantly education – are constructed by a male dominated society. Boys are not just 'being boys', they are being the boys we tell them to be. We can both show and teach them how to be something different, something better.

CHAPTER 6

Enablers

What are the enablers that accelerate sexual violence and encourage or fail to prevent the factors that feed or fuel it? The most obvious is the invisibility and silence that surrounds the issue. The light shone on the common experience of sexual violence by many women through #MeToo, brought home that there was nowhere else to tell of their traumatic experiences.

INVISIBILITY

> "Non reporting is rife, and is usually rational and justifiable."
>
> (297)

The World Health Organisation estimates that one in three women experience physical/sexual violence during their lifetime (21) but this often quoted prevalence rate does not include sexual harassment. Rates do vary across countries, cultures, ethnicity, age, gender and sexual identity but what does not vary is that the majority do not report it (298). This silent majority includes the 85% of sexual offences not disclosed to the authorities in the UK (12).

Despite the significant impacts on physical and mental health (214), most do not get help after a sexual assault, many disclosing much later when the harms of hidden trauma emerge (216,298,299). Within the context of a low level of reporting we can begin to see a picture of trauma remaining silent, hidden and untreated, with worldwide the consequences of sexual assault and rape recognised as a significant public health burden (227). In combination with wider male violence against women and girls, the UN have described a 'shadow pandemic' alongside that of COVID 19 (300). For obvious reasons, finding out who remains silent is almost impossible (301); what we do know is that most do not tell formal agencies who may record

DOI: 10.4324/9781003168591-7

rates, such as the police (302). Even with this gaping hole, crime statistics are often referenced by politicians to evidence current 'need' (303). There is a gap at the heart of our understanding of sexual violence and harm, erasing so many people's experience of trauma.

Various rates from a range of sources echo the 'most don't tell' message but the hidden nature of sexual violence amongst the young may be even greater. US universities have to carry out surveys on sexual violence by law (115), they find between 95% and 72% of victim/survivors did not disclose (304) and 48% of those sexually assaulted as children did not tell anyone (305). Being young is a risk factor for victimisation and not disclosing, but also the nature of the incident plays a role. Stranger attacks using physical violence fit societies' 'rape myth' stereotype (28). Many women will only try to report to the police incidents which fall within narrow perception of rape because of fear of not being believed (306). Current estimates show less than one in six females suffering rape report to the police (200). African American women are even less likely to tell, with the expectation (based on experience) that racist services will not listen (197). Victims' silence mirrors the landscape of subordination in our societies and is secured using specific tools of shame and blame. To understand the complex experience of this we need to listen to and hear the voices and value the stories of victim/survivors.

SILENCING VOICES OF BLAME AND SHAME

> "It was fear that stopped me going straight to the police. Fear and I think, a deep kind of shock. I didn't want this to have happened to me. I didn't want to believe it had. . . . I told K I hadn't been raped. . . . I moved into the bottom of a well and I stayed there a long time."
>
> (307)

Not telling can be both conscious, wanting to avoid shame or blame, but also unconscious. Studies show that coerced sex, generally (90%) by someone you know (205) is not a clear-cut experience to describe, even if the traumatic impact of assault is very deeply felt by the victim (299) and up to 60% of women (308) and perhaps even more men (201) may not acknowledge a rape. Historically, sexual abuse has been defined using 'he said she said', criminal justice framing of 'evidence' (69). This is in stark contrast to the nuanced and often non-verbal nature of the experience of sexual abuse and violence (44).

Survey data on sexual assault at US university campuses shows 50% of victims reported that they said nothing as they were confused about what had happened and 40% felt they couldn't as they had been drinking or using drugs, so were fearful of being blamed or were already blaming themselves (304). Our own research with student victim/survivors of a range of sexual harassment and abuse speaks to a period of initial confusion and processing particularly in relation to betrayal from a friend, partner or acquaintance,

> "I didn't recognise it as sexual assault for quite some time. I kind of viewed it as me cocking up and y'know things happening."
>
> (307)

> "I doubted and played down the events after they happened."
>
> (107)

This struggle with 'sense making' extends to the labels available to define their experience (309):

> "I still have an issue with calling it rape. I feel like that's not the word for it . . . it's a loaded term isn't it? I don't know why I have such an issue calling a spade a spade. Did I consent or no?"
>
> (307)

What is often the most natural survival reaction to a traumatic event, freezing or tonic immobility (310), makes it hard for victims not to blame themselves for what they should have done. These stereotypes about how people should behave or report in order to appear credible, run through the criminal justice system (311).

> "I asked him to stop and he wouldn't. I asked him multiple times and he just got rougher. I froze and just let him do it."
>
> (7)

> "It was like somebody turned off the lights on my whole body" or "Being captured inside myself."
>
> (312)

The belief that those experiencing sexual violence should have done more to prevent it compounds the internal struggle to make sense and name the experience, let alone report it (309). The impact of being traumatised and the enduring nature of the post-traumatic state render short reporting timescales impossible for many (313). Widespread acceptance of rape myths ensure a lack of relatable narratives and terms, time frame and reactions. Other research reports that acknowledging sexual assault can be harmful for some but adaptive for others (309).

"Not all sexual violence is violent and that can make it difficult to relate to the term."

(307)

Confusion and fear of blame or shame are not unfounded. High profile incidents such as the testimony of Dr Christine Blasey-Ford (13) paint a clear picture of the personal cost of telling, a cost that currently seems to outweigh the potential benefit. We can see why the UN felt it important to point out that 'not telling' is a rational choice (297), but what happens when you do reach a point of disclosing?

Most will eventually tell someone, in younger women first disclosure is often made informally to a friend or relative (314). Older women are more likely to tell a mental health professional within therapy in later life (299). The first time they open up is often in the context of trying to treat the impact it has had on their lives through psychological distress, ongoing PTSD or addiction (299). In general, those close enough to be trusted with the disclosure such as family and friends, often mirror the rape myths that inform popular understanding of sexual abuse (313). Negative reactions such as 'did you have a drink' or 'he seems such a nice guy' put the blame back on the victim. At the same time, a reaction of 'trying to help' that pushes victims to formally report, can also cause harm (315). Studies show that responses that focus on the role of the victim or victim shaming, shut down telling and block the possibility that victims get to services, thereby amplifying PTSD (299,313). Victim/survivors may further withdraw and try and cope on their own or experience external help as further loss of control (299).

Where do these expectations of what sexual violence looks and feels like come from? Society expects a certain type of scenario in sexual assault which the research shows us exclude the range of responses to trauma such as staying in touch with the perpetrator.

RAPE MYTHS

The existence of rape myths across many cultures is well established and these myths speak to three basic ideas: sexual violence was the fault of the victim; perpetuators are therefore not to blame or erased from the picture; and sexual violence itself is not a serious issue, just 'sex gone bad', 'regretted' and maybe should be taken as a compliment (315).

The Fawcett Society asked 'if a women goes out late at night, wearing a short skirt, gets drunk, and is then the victim of a sexual assault, is she totally or partly to blame?', 38% of all men and 34% of all women said that she was and this tendency to blame increased with the age of the person asked (316). It is, therefore not surprising that if rape myths are commonly held, they can be seen in the perpetrator's own narrative in carrying out acts of sexual violence (317) and are expressed through the structures set up to respond including juries failing to convict (268).

> "Everything is always the girls fault, she can prevent it, you were either asking for it or whatever." Lucy
>
> (85)

In this quote, Lucy is saying victim blaming is normal and it certainly frames police safety messages, something the research literature confirms (318). These are directed almost exclusively at women and girls, focusing on the need for them to do the right thing, go to the right places and wear the right clothes or save themselves by 'flagging down a bus' (319). This 'safety work' is seen as the responsibility of women (231).

> "It's never boys . . . let's have a discussion about how not to harass women." Grace
>
> (85)

In other words the message is sexual bullying or violence can only be avoided by women giving up freedoms.

For racially minoritised women and girls there is a greater lack of trust around how authorities will deal with any complaint based on previous experience of racism (183). There is evidence of greater reliance on stereotypes such as racialised forms of hyper-sexualisation of Black women's bodies (190) and common reframing of sexual abuse as 'cultural' (183). Victims may face pressure to protect perpetrators as a way of resisting lived experience of racism from criminal justice agencies (186). Minoritised women may be silenced both by the inequality inside their communities and from outside in the responses of formal agencies. The racism justice gap extends to other groups (LGBTQ+, disabled people) whose experience does not fit the rape myth ideal and are therefore, less served by the justice system. They are more invisible because they have even less power (191) which is often framed as individual vulnerability rather than structural inequality (320). If the pattern of perpetration and the corresponding lack of consequences delineates a picture of exclusion and marginalisation, how is sexual violence not about power?

Initial confusion about sexual violence may be partly driven by the chasm between what 'actually happened' and what rape myths say 'should have happened'. Victim/survivors speak of a need to have their experience validated by the perpetrator, family/friends and or police/society, to acknowledge that they have been wronged (241). In depriving sexual violence victims of a narrative, words for and recognition of what happened to them, we are depriving them of the tools of recovery. The process of telling and retelling what they have lived through, sharing that experience and having it acknowledged heals trauma and holds the cure. Silence ensures it remains poisonous (214,321).

> "You can't really heal, if you can't talk about what you need to talk about, you can't heal properly." Anna
>
> (240)

How are these norms of aggressive sexual behaviour taught? To understand the tools that enable a narrative where it is okay to ignore an individual's rights over their own body, we have to look at representations of sex and the spread of access to aggressive porn that degrades the humanity of women.

PORN PROSECCO

It is easy to find evidence of the mainstreaming of imagery and norms of pornography, this also may include normalising sexually aggressive hair pulling, eroticised degradation, strangulation rape/incest plots and absence of meaningful consent (166). One in eight videos promoted by online porn sites to first time users carry titles the WHO defines as acts of sexual violence (266). It is just fantasy right?

With increasing access, the narrative of porn has spread into mainstream culture (322) from fashion advertising and public spaces (American Apparel advertising leg warmers on a naked girl) to food ('Porn Star' Prosecco sold in Marks and Spencer). It would be an oversimplification of a complex relationship to suggest that solitary males, consuming violent pornography lead to society wide increases in sexual violence. We should consider its role in enabling a narrative in which 'rough sex' can be offered as a defence against violent murder of a women by her sexual partner (323).

The Children's Commissioner for England carried out an overview of the evidence; it was starkly entitled – 'Basically . . . porn is everywhere' (1). From this report we know that through increased internet and mobile phone use, pornography is now highly accessible at a younger age. Some studies report significant numbers of children being exposed (generally accidentally) at approximately 10 or 11 years of age (324,325). Rates of exposure for young people across the world have been reported from 43 per cent to 99 per cent, with exposure and access higher in boys and points of exposure around transition to secondary school or earlier (1).

We also know that porn content focusing on male sexual aggression is more accessible, one study back in 2010 found 88% of scenes included physical aggression, overwhelmingly directed against women (326) and more recent studies confirm the common theme of sexual violence in porn (266).

Women are shown responding to such sexual aggression with neutrality or pleasure (326,327). Content involves key scripts around force/violence, lack of consent and sexualised teens as well as routinely making available non-consensual image abuse material (328) such as 'upskirting' videos (53).

The most robust form of evidence, systematic reviews of all the available studies, point to the central script within porn of gender inequality (327). The interplay of males 'assumed right' versus females 'awaited permission' is clearly a problem. This provides porn consumers with a story line of men needing to overcome women's passivity or resistance. Trying to prove or disprove a generalised direct causal relationship is a red herring and fails to capture the complexity of porn's multifaceted relationship to sexual aggression. We need to understand how, in groups with pre-existing vulnerabilities (see Chapter 5), porn may fuel sexual violence. Perhaps more importantly, it provides bad sex education and drip feeds a background of toxic, gender stereotypical sexual norms (166) in which sexual abuse becomes wallpaper. Both young men and women are having their sexual expectations shaped by commercial vested interests and a profit-driven industry exploiting a new, all encompassing, online world (166).

How does porn inform the norms of sexual behaviour? Research into police cases on sexual violence cited instances of boys and young men directly referring pornography during sexual assaults:

> "It was like being in a porn film."
>
> (329)

Snap shot surveys of large groups (cross sectional studies) show that young people do learn sexual behaviours from watching porn (330) and that they also feel pressure to imitate what it depicts (331). Porn use is not only normalised or increasingly considered acceptable but even expected (327). Without high quality, balanced sex education such as that provided by programs such as 'It's Time We Talked' (332) or Tender (www.tender.org.uk), porn acts as a bad sex educator for many. For some, sexually aggressive distortions can interact with existing vulnerability, a causal pathway that may also mean less access to protective 'buffers' such as good sex education and family openness about sex (151,263,333). Again, A does not necessarily lead to B: existing vulnerability may lead to young people seeking out more extreme content (265) and we need to be careful about the direction of causality. Research trying to distinguish between the two favours the mediating role of sexual attitudes in communicating sexually aggressive norms (261) through bad sex education (266,334). For others, it may help meet a need to see sexual violence or dehumanising women as normal (335). What is clearer is porn's contribution to the wider cultural context and the expectation that men take and women are available to be taken (1,114,266,335). We have less evidence from those perpetuating acts of sexual bullying. @Emma Barnett on Radio 4 invited men who cat call in the street to get in touch on her radio show, one caller said:

> "I haven't got children. Women to me are just objects."

We need to acknowledge the complexity of the interaction between porn and sexual violence and abuse, rather than a misleading polemic of good/ bad. Yes, there is harm, a comprehensive review of 20 years of research around the links between pornography and behaviour has shown effects on both genders with use linked to greater sexual aggression as well as higher perpetration and victimisation (265).

A valuable and comprehensive model of sexual violence factors by the EU Commission illuminates pathways by which devaluing women, rigid definitions of masculinity and legal impunity for violence against women can combine with depersonalised norms of sex and intimacy deficits to create the conditions for sexual abuse and violence (114).

Part of the failure to understand the role of pornography in sexual violence is the simplicity of the maps we use. Trying to connect dots of individuals or instances of sexual violence through crime statistics and rape cases is a failure to recognise the patterns and understand the landscape of sexual bullying as a defence mechanism (273). A recent review of rape prosecutions clearly made this link by calling for an end to rape and sexual abuse as commercial entertainment and the proliferation of violent pornography as consumers may both internalise and see affirmation in, the sexual norms they show (311). Understanding cultural normalisation of sexual aggression is only one side of the story, seeing how this manifests in structures is the other. We have a criminal justice system that defines rape as illegal but fails to prosecute or secure convictions (336,337) as if it doesn't matter.

LEGAL IMMUNITY

The vast majority of men in an international study who admitted rape did not face any legal consequences (269)

> "Because the men were so much older than me, they knew that they scared me and that I would not do anything about their behaviour, which in turn meant that they knew they could continue to get away with what they were doing."
>
> (87)

Historically, politicians have underestimated the scope of victimisation behind the #MeToo movement, relying instead on quoting the formal reporting of sexual violence offences to evidence a decline in rates rather than a decline in reporting (303). The UK's Crown Prosecution Service data show that in the year ending March 2017, 3,671 cases were charged, by 2020 this had fallen to 1,867, a 50% cut (338). Yet the total number of rapes reported between 2014 to 2018 had tripled from 20,751 up to 53,970 (12). The latest data show that fewer than 1 in 70 rape cases recorded by police in 2020 resulted in a charge let alone a court case or conviction (336). More recently a UK government report has acknowledged that the system is failing victims and that they were 'extremely sorry' (337).

We have a justice system therefore that is failing to even prosecute sexual violence let alone convict in a court with a jury (338). Good research evidence shows that those juries, in being made up of lay members of our society, bring with them a 'rape myth' based understanding of what sexual abuse/violence should look like (268). What they see in real cases does not match what they expect from rape such as knowing the perpetrator, freezing or appeasing vs fighting back, delayed reporting, trauma memory selectivity and consistent, rational behaviour (339). The gap between expectations and reality persists despite Crown Prosecution detailed guidance to prosecutors around how to negate rape myths (340) and the Crown Bench book 2011 for judges (341) for directing juries away from such commonly held misconceptions.

Empathy for the male accused may well be hard wired in our society (342) and even has a name, 'himpathy' (5). We pay attention to the impact on the male accused first because we are likely to hear more about it and therefore it is more concrete, designated after the fact and in the form of criminal justice punishment (5). A CNN reporter in covering a 2013 conviction for rape in the US reported,

> "Incredibly difficult, even for an outsider like me, to watch what happened as these two young men that had such promising futures, star football players, very good students, literally watched as they believed their lives fell apart."
>
> (343)

This plays out in a reluctance of juries to convict perpetrators even if they believe a serious sexual assault has been committed (344).

This empathy gap extends to the general public's belief that sexual violence is rare, often falsely alleged, only happens in isolated, easily avoidable (by the victim) or doesn't happen 'here' as they have not seen it (345).

> "(Men) don't see it they don't think it happens." Ffion, 25
>
> (85)

In contrast, the impact on victims, who are generally silent or less heard, cannot be seen or, therefore, empathised with. The pain is endured silently or is simply invisible, women's accounts on #MeToo came from the silence of the pain bearers. We do hear much more about women's role in avoiding and potential blame for sexual abuse (66). The '#NoMoreRapeMyths' campaigning group from Nottinghamshire Sexual Violence Support Services promotes responsible reporting, challenging media coverage on the issue of sexual violence. They call out examples in which male agency is rendered invisible in reporting sexual violence such as 'Two girls, 15, "raped at Australian holiday resort" after meeting 3 men on New Year's Eve' (346).

Male agency within rape trials is also less visible as evidence around past sexual history is commonly used against female complainants; three-quarters of trials refer to the victim's sexual history despite the 1990 Act to minimise its use (347). Sexual history is used to feed ideas around promiscuity, showing a woman has had sex before means her consent is therefore more likely (348). Minimising or 'smoothing' violence happens through language that frames repeated groping as 'romantic persistence', stalking as 'being in love' (349) or even murder as 'rough sex gone wrong' (323). In effect, current evidential thresholds for rape victims to be believed are impossible:

> "They must have perfect recollection of the alleged assault and report it immediately; they must not have been drinking; they must not have had consensual sex with their attacker at any point before the assault; they must not have exchanged friendly or sexual messages."
>
> (350)

We see men as credible but women's accounts are dismissed or worse, turned against them (351). The cost to men's lives, potential, careers and wellbeing are just more important (5). The UK government's own review states that the victim is the one investigated on reporting sexual assault in order to establish her credibility rather than his offending behaviour or history rendering the criminal justice option, 'almost like a fortress that you can't get through' as described by one complainant (337).

Criminal justice systems can be experienced as harmful and re-traumatising, compounding the pain of the sexual abuse suffered. For what, when even those reporting to the police face only a 1 in 70 chance of even getting a formal charge (311). Victim/survivors can be faced with the dilemma of pursuing their case or recovering but not both.

A tripling of reported rapes since 2012 set against a steady drop in prosecutions and convictions for rape represents not only a "dramatic decline" (337) but systemic discrimination against women (311).

This treatment does not occur only within the legal system, it is an expression of the cultural scaffolding of permission society gives perpetrators by making victims invisible and explaining toxic male domination as 'nature'. Women are permitted limited sexual agency as the gatekeepers of their own safety but men are depicted as unable to control their own sexual response (352) or violence (206). The rest of us bystanders, well we just don't say anything. Women speak of a double burden of suffering traumatic sexual abuse and then facing a justice system that compounds that abuse.

> "There was this idea that maybe it was my fault that I didn't get justice. . . .
> I was able to put the responsibility where it belongs, with the perpetrator
> and the institutions that support them instead of supporting us."
>
> (240)

Depictions of sexual bullying/harassment, violence and abuse are not based in wider social inequality but tend to focus on the acts of victims and perpetrators and this may be partly functional. The studies around empathy for male perpetrators over female victims suggest that social identity (who we think we are and who we compare ourselves to) might be playing a role. The way we police our social boundaries about what is 'normal' and how we feel safe by distancing threat as something that happens to people not like us, drives us to make both victim and perpetrator 'other' (178). The 'isolated incident' approach to systemic abuse saves us from having to see the 'next door' nature of sexual violence which is harder to look at. How close to home does it have to get before we see the threat? The stories we tell ourselves about male sex drive and lone monster perpetrators gives many a comfortable distance (255) but #MeToo revealed it was often someone we knew.

BOYS WILL BE BOYS

Agency in sexual harassment and abuse has been shown to split along lines of gender with a 'boys being boys' narrative of inevitable male sexual aggression (352) whilst girls are seen as pathological if they demonstrate sexual agency (353). The 'boys will be boys' excuse can be seen as both a display of masculinity through 'lad culture' (or frat culture in the US) (354) and society's erasing of the harm of sexual aggression, something often internalised by victim/survivors (355). 'Lad culture' is often represented in the press as synonymous with performance behaviour of male sports clubs or students at university, initiation ceremonies for societies, 'pimps and hoes' parties (120). It is a kind of benevolent indulgence or cleansing of offensive sexist, racist or homophobic behaviour, reframing it as the way young men bond through pack drinking, sport and 'banter'.

Within this frame, sexual aggression is read as biologically determined or set in stone and driven by rigid patterns of establishing masculine prowess/masculine norms (269). The work of Karen Lorimer in Glasgow (285) shows how these pathways to status are magnified where other routes are less available (areas of high poverty) or may be exaggerated in environments where young people are learning how to become adults such as in Higher Education (120). At the same time, data is clear that most men don't but, more than this, most men also don't call it out (356) or as Tim Winton described it, they don't take responsibility for the 'constant pressure to enlist, to pull on the uniform of misogyny and join the Shithead Army that enforces and polices sexism' (357).

All this in the face of women's experiences of wall-to-wall harassment,

> "I could list hundreds of other individual incidents: a man walked past me in a shop and put his hand up my dress and grabbed my crotch. A group of men loudly marked me out of ten as I walked past. A man in a nightclub dragged me into the men's toilets to 'get it on' as his friends watched and laughed. Being followed home late at night. Being followed in broad daylight . . . every one of my female friends could do the same."
>
> (358)

There is a particular need to look beyond the nearest bystander (see Chapter 4) to male bystanders and their male peers. 'Lad culture' plays into acts of perpetration and not calling them out in others unless it is to frame victims' reactions as a failure to take a compliment or a joke (359,360).

> "He was like, 'Well I can't do anything about that, you should feel flattered'."
>
> (8)

> "It's not a compliment when somebody screams at you from a moving car, and then switches round and comes back, it just doesn't feel like a compliment to me."
>
> (8)

Wider 'lad' reactions to acts of perpetration effectively 'gaslight' victim/survivors' experience as a misunderstanding on their part or 'making mountains out of molehills or political correctness by a "liberal elite"' (361).

As #MeToo progressed we began to see faux confusion from some men around how to navigate new boundaries of correct behaviour, some newspaper headlines read 'Is hugging still OK?' (362). The idea that the line is so difficult to see has been effectively addressed in satirical comedy.

> "'Are you a creep? Do you touch women without being invited? Do you say things to make women squirm? Have you forced a woman to engage in sexual activity with you?' No? You are probably ok."
>
> (363)

Listening and believing the lived experience of victim/survivors means, if it feels creepy, it is creepy. It feels like the opposite of a compliment or attraction, it feels like contempt (364). Their stories have value.

STRANGE LINES IN THE NATURE OF CONSENT

"The ways consent can be stolen and the strange lines between liberation and exploitation."

(221)

Micheala Coel, author of a dramatisation that draws on her own sexual assault, talks about 'the theft of consent' more commonly experienced in initially consensual sexual experiences as "halfway through 'sometimes it is like a magic trick and it leaves the person thinking 'how did that happen' but knowing that 'something feels wrong'" (221).

The majority of sexual violence victim/survivors know their assailant (90%) (205) and the morphing of an initially consensual relationship into one of abuse can compound confusion.

"You don't associate rape with a couple of close friends."

(307)

That someone they trusted could hurt them and betray them, will often lead them to question their own contribution or focus on their own blame:

"I had a history of being slightly promiscuous I guess you'd say, so I just kind of thought oh well, this is what you get."

(307)

Why? because they have been taught to do so and do not recognise the definition of rape or sexual violence as describing what happened to them.

"I suppose it's coming to realise that not all sexual violence is about bruises . . . the reason I'm wary of [rape] and talk more about consent . . . is because I guess I feel like I have no recollection of what happened. Could I have consented? Could I have given the come on? Potentially. Is that rape? The lines are so murky . . . it's a difficult term to relate to."

(307)

US research on consent suggested that women do not feel they have the 'right to say no', whereas men just feel they have the 'right' to sex (365).

Further work suggests that men rely on non-verbal cues for consent while women rely more on verbal (366) hence there is an inevitable mismatch. Consent, or lack of it, communicated through a mixture of behaviour and verbal cues requires someone else's interpretation of an implied yes or no with little or no verbal confirmation (366). Messaging from porn has already laid out the script in which any form of 'no' can be ignored. A 'no' when translated into the criminal justice language of what was said and done can seem very straightforward and memory may well be clouded by drugs, alcohol or trauma, but most of us can easily recognise when something feels wrong (367).

Blurring of 'wanting to have sex' with 'feeling you have to agree to sex' can be unpacked through recognising the circumstances in which women agree to have sex they do not want: to avoid a row, to keep a job, to de-escalate the threat of violence; or to get out alive (368). Sexual consent is also generally an evolving, mutual process that can change at any point, not a one-off decision (367,369). This makes sense when thinking about the most common sexual harassment/abuse realities of existing friendship, acquaintance, partner relationships. Traditionally, the male asks and the female refuses sex but this is then seen as an invitation to try harder (370). How traditional? "you are not serious in your rejection of me, I shall choose to attribute it to your wish of increasing my love by suspense, according to the usual practice of elegant females." Mr Collins in *Pride and Prejudice* by Jane Austen, on handling rejection (371).

Studies show that men see women's initial refusal as necessary in order not to appear 'easy' and therefore, he has to overcome this or 'just wear her down' (372). The idea pervades sexual scripts across cultures in which we are teaching men to ignore no. In turn, outright rejection brings its own risks. Women must somehow find the perfect balance between a 'no that means no', without it giving offence, such as 'I already have a boyfriend', a message that replicates masculine honour beliefs, and the problem itself (373).

Definitions of consent implied in active affirmative 'yes' campaigns (372) or even 'no means no' may not take into account the reality of consent such as using passive resistance as rejection (366). How can victim/survivors hope to understand or even label non-consensual sex, set against a rigid plot of strangers, dark alleys and physical violence rather than the reality of boyfriends, friends or even family.

Within ideas of consent, we do need to flag up sex workers and how everything considered so far can translate into the normalisation of women as objects or rentable property. How does consent sit within transactional sex? Without going into the depth this area deserves, we can connect the fact that sexual violence relates to framing of women as consumable objects or property to be owned within marriage (114). However, consent is about choice and overviews of the evidence (374) illustrate the common experience of sex work as survival based, coming from a place where choice is limited and therefore consent 'ceremonial'. Population surveys have found that the acceptability of 'illegal prostitution' (their term) is connected to acceptability of sexual harassment (24).

Gendered and contradictory understandings of what consent is speaks of different worlds of sex education, one informed by 'Disney' princesses, the other by early exposure to aggressive porn. It is harder for females to have their own 'sexual project' or agency (44) with a sexual relationship as a goal. These plots permit both sexual abuse perpetration and immunity but fail to make the connections to gender inequality. For that we need a bigger map.

THE MAPS WE USE

The picture we get from both hard evidence of prevalence and listening to women's experience is that sexual harassment and violence is every day and next door. In contrast, incidents are treated as just that, isolated, individual one-offs, perpetuated by 'monsters' from a bad family (375). Monsters are easily condemned as different, not to do with normal people like us. This failure to connect or acknowledge the common patterns of sexual violence to the social norms we teach young people and model ourselves, means the maps we use to make sense of sexual violence simply don't work to stop it. They ensure the wider status and power inequalities are not framed as causal. The 'monster/isolated incident myth' is a comforting illusion that stops us having to examine the male dominated society we have constructed (255,376).

Maps are often criminal justice led and yet we have seen that most victim/survivors will experience sexual harassment, abuse and violence without any reference to the criminal justice system (298).

An 'ecological' model or understanding people in the context of how they relate to each other, their surroundings, their family, community and society allows us to look at the causes of sexual violence across multiple layers (20,114). Once we start to recognise patterns, we can also begin to build a prevention approach using the evidence base of what works (114). That includes addressing wider determinants or upstream causes of sexual violence (377) and moving beyond criminal justice sanctions (280) to prevention.

We have allowed society to frame sexual violence within the imperative of male sex drive and reciprocal female submission and objectification (166). This impacts a range of less powerful groups including women but also deeply harms men and boys (152). The theoretical maps can be seen across our media depictions of sexual entitlement (378) where sexual violence is so normal we don't even register it anymore (379). Mass communication's representation of sexual violence reflects back these maps and entertainment media content, for example, crime dramas, often regurgitate traditional rape myths (380). One female writer recalls:

> "Someone always suggested a character get raped. I said, 'the thing is, that character's already been raped.' There was this big silence, and my boss said, 'When was she last raped?' "
>
> (381)

A French crime drama's opening scene sees a male prosecutor talking about a graphically pictured, mutilated, naked female victim/not survivor, he concludes "I am sure she was beautiful . . . they killed her for her beauty" (382). The author, Raymond Chandler recalled "if you're worried that nobody's really feeling it, kill a woman" (381). Dramatisation of violence and sexual violence against women varies wildly from Happy Valley's rape survivor's overt resistance to being defined by her experience; "What happened says more about him than it'll ever say about me" (383) to The Fall's misleading narrative of a 'hot rapist' (384). The Investigation (385) worked closely with family members to create an account of the murder of Kim Wall, a journalist, without naming the perpetrator or describing the details of the crime, it gave a real sense of who that person was in life and the impact of her loss. If an act of perpetration or its depiction equate to an act of victim erasure, responsible portrayal should put the victim or survivor at the heart of an account.

It would be simplistic to blame male 'gaze' and industry viewing statistics show more women watch crime drama (386). Attempts to understand gendered motives for watching dramatised sexual violence has suggested a male need to study how to protect women and a female need to explore their own victimisation (387). More worryingly, fetishising dead women's bodies may contribute to its normalisation; two policemen were arrested for circulating pictures of Bibaa Henry and her sister Nicola Smallman after they were murdered having celebrated a friend's birthday in a park (388).

Insiders (389) say gendered depictions of sexual violence are being changed through diversity and female writers' voices are more heard in writers rooms. This moves us forward to the most likely tool of prevention in which diversity acts as a teacher. By taking a broad-brush approach to what causes sexual violence we open up a greater range of tools to prevent it.

CHAPTER 7

Hope – prevention

If we have understood anything so far it is that perpetration of sexual violence/abuse and the way society ignores it are learnt behaviours informed by social norms (20). They are choices and therefore, we can simply choose to do this in another way. Sexual harassment and abuse are preventable (390). There are a range of ways it can and has been tackled and we have an evidence base to guide us. Good intentions are not enough. We cannot present a picture of societal level drivers and then attempt to 'arrest' our way out of sexual violence and abuse through measures that kick in after the fact of individual acts (269). There are three fundamental starting points to a prevention strategy: understand the prevalence; use the evidence of what has worked; and situate this within an ecological map of cause to harness theory of what may work. I would add, start from and listen to those with lived experience. No one measure will achieve this, we have to address diversity in our society and its expression in our organisations but we also have to tackle social norms through education, training as well as more responsible media coverage and regulation for harm prevention. This may feel overwhelming, but start at the data, shine a light on how much it happens by encouraging reporting. We need to respond better with existing, but under-used, tools of enforcement and a wider range of compassionate, trauma-informed and causation aware laws and treatment programmes to benefit survivors and to de-escalate perpetration. Central to these responsibilities is unlocking the role of men. Sexual harassment and abuse is not a 'women's issue', neither is it helpful to frame it as a 'man's problem'; this comes down to negotiating how we live together as a community.

What do we know so far? Work that draws individual studies together, looks at the relative contribution of each depending on the quality of the science and reads across the piece to synthesise gaps and promising next steps (systematic reviews) helps. Reviews find plenty of studies but many that are too small, do not effectively measure real world change or do not

DOI: 10.4324/9781003168591-8

use study design to pick out the 'active ingredients'. Most of them examine single interventions (391), many measure success by what people thought of the programme. Some move on to measuring if attitudes shifted but it is extremely rare to measure actual change in behaviour six months, or one year down the line. Take the example of prevention of sexual violence perpetration; Sarah DeGue and her colleagues examined 140 studies of programmes and interventions. Only three were found to be effective in moving beyond changing attitudes such as rape myths (definitely a move in the right direction) to the next step of reducing sexually violent behaviour (139). In other words bridging the 'knowing–doing' gap. Widely delivered 'bystander' programmes can change beliefs in individuals' own ability and intention to do something and increase the rate by which they do step in (392) but evidence of their impact on sexual violence itself has not been demonstrated; some promising single study based results have been achieved through bystander programmes such as Green Dot in the US (www.livethegreendot.com).

Other initiatives such as adding a gender-based offence to hate crime, have little evidence in terms of real life impact as yet (such as increased reporting) (8) and yet there have been nationwide calls to introduce this (393). This illustrates an evidence/policy gap (394), something that can be bridged by theory. Unless you can describe how you think something is going to work, it can mean very little to pick out markers for success to try and prove it. Articulating a theory of how A leads to B in a 'theory of change' is the only way to show change is improvement rather than just activity. At the same time, it allows us to understand how A unexpectedly led to Z or other unintended consequences. Such multi-level maps have been described in a way to include complex, messy factors (114).

The existing evidence is concentrated on individual level predictors of abuse, we have less to go on for community or structural change (391) even though we know intervention needs to happen at all these levels (20). The evidence we do have tends to measure success against 'buckets' of change such as all forms of violence against women and girls (domestic, sexual) or within global south settings (reading across low and middle income countries). Fair evidence exists on the usefulness of group-based work including mixed gender groups, healthy relationships work, school education for boys and young men (Stepping Stones (395)); or micro-finance programmes alongside gender transformative work (IMAGE (396)); community level social norms programmes and combinations of this with group work or parenting programmes. Further evidence (397) looks beyond what to do to address how to do it and highlights the need for multicomponent activities of education, persuasion, modelling and enablement; multi-level programming that mobilises wider communities: targeting both men and women; and programmes of longer duration. Some key characteristics stand out, for example, programmes that include healthy views of masculinity and relationships (gender transformative) are generally more promising (397). The WHO sets out seven levels of comprehensive action using the acronym RESPECT, Relationships and skills, Empowerment of women, Services, Poverty reduction, Environment as a focus, Child and adolescent abuse (school-based dating violence prevention) and Transform attitudes beliefs and norms (390). Less useful are standalone or one-off awareness raising events, brief bystander training or victim focused safety planning for pregnant women (398). A real gap exists around what we know works for diverse/more targeted groups or more complex interventions. The basic message is that one thing, in one place with one group is not enough.

We need to use evaluation to ensure that the limited resources given to sexual violence prevention are spent on the best possible programmes and across all levels from societal, cultural to policy and practice (397). Perhaps more importantly, work should 'do no harm'. There is some evidence (although not systematic) that workplace sexual harassment and diversity training can increase harm. In a study of 800 U.S. companies between the 1970s and the early 2000s, the training and grievance procedures around sexual harassment did not work in reducing sexual harassment prevalence and were seen to increase female workers' disaffection and turnover (399). This study used an important theory-based outcome measure that recognised the common harassment avoidance coping strategy for many women was leaving. Common 'backlash' or resistance responses may be to blame and have been evidenced in reactions to diversity training (400). Maybe that is the problem: telling people to promote diversity within a structure that does not model it. At the same time, little evidence has shown that commonly employed and universally recommended organisational policy rewrites make any difference (401), probably because no one checks (no evaluation studies).

MODEL IT – DIVERSITY

Power and intersectional exclusion from that power, create places of work, study and public spaces that are not equally open to and do not represent, women (391) or others such as the racially minoritised, people with disabilities or non-conforming and LGBTQ+ groups.

The concept of intersectionality and how this can play out through layers of 'who I am as a woman, as a black person as gay person' connects us to related issues. Conroy Harris of Band of Brothers (a charity to support positive social change for men), talks about the 'safety work' of black men and how they have to plan and accommodate racially profiled law enforcement when going out in public (402), a behaviour that mirrors that of women's 'safety work' to avoid sexual harassment/abuse in public spaces (231). Even today, efforts to explain the results of structural inequality such as racial health inequality as the impact of systemic racism, are resisted (403) or reimagined as in the Report of the Commission on Racial Disparities in which phrases such as 'structural racism' are described as only to be used 'when deep-seated racism can be proven on a systemic level' (404).

Macpherson's definition of structural racism from the inquiry into the death of Stephen Lawrence demands repetition, often, in full and equally describes sex discrimination.

> "The collective failure of an organisation to provide an appropriate and professional service to people because of their colour, culture or ethnic origin. It can be seen or detected in processes, attitudes and behaviour which amount to discrimination through unwitting prejudice, ignorance, thoughtlessness and racial stereotyping."
>
> (39)

We just need to add gender. We have seen that commonly used stand-alone training will not work but actual diversity is a more promising teacher (140). Sexual bullying is a civil rights issue where hierarchies of age, money, race, ethnicity and gender are supported by legal, media and religious scaffolding that reinforce social norms of men being superior to women (405). One woman's description of the impact of sexual harassment resonates here.

> "I no longer run freely round the city I live in. I ruminate on the harassment – I work with statistics and so try to find patterns in the harassment. The pattern for me goes something like this: Early mornings have fewer people, and so fewer harassers. But the early morning harassment (masturbation, threats, following) has been of a more alarming and focused type. One pre-sunrise shouted threat stopped me running in [location] for months. Evenings have fewer lone men. And it's busier, but harassing men in groups of two or more seem to favour getting into my path and blocking my way, along with wordless heckling. I'll run into the road to get around them. And I've been masturbated at in the evening too. In the daytime it seems more unpredictable: more shouting from van or car windows, more tooting, some truly bloodcurdling harassment."
>
> (406)

Diversity may be effective through simply having different perspectives 'in the room' as the historian David Olusoga, describes in relation to diversity and racism:

> "Being the only black person . . . means being the only person asking certain questions, the only person uncomfortable that an image or a sequence reinforces certain stereotypes."
>
> (407)

A study of the experience of black students at predominantly white universities sums up the effect of minoritisation; "You never feel so Black as when you're contrasted against a White background" (408). The impact of not seeing yourself in the people around or leading you is allied to that of gender discrimination. Review studies and global policy around violence against women and girls (390), health (409) and the workforce (410) show the potential of real diversity through changing attitudes and growing skills.

So why are standalone, workplace diversity training courses that do not work and may cause harm (411,412) still used? Diversity training that does not make intersectional or structural inequality connections (413), seems to be designed as a duty of care, 'sticking plaster' to protect the organisation with a 'we did all we could' legal defence (412) in order to minimise liability (414). Pointing to training alone as an act of prevention is just cynical as are tokenistic claims of 'taking it seriously' showing 'zero tolerance'.

The overall gender pay gap stands at 15.5% and is particularly acute for women in their 40s and 50s (415). Women make up only 6% of FTSE 100 Chief Executive Officers (none are women of colour), 21% of national newspaper editors and 34% of Members of Parliament (416). Women are more than twice as likely as men to be sexual harassed in the workplace (92) and yet, in the UK, there is no published strategy to tackle gender-based inequality (137). The Government Equalities Office (GEO) has no formal role in overseeing the work of government and no function in looking at how inequalities intersect (137). What is the role of government and legal structures?

There are laws, international and domestic, that should, if enforced, promote and protect equity (417). International agreements such as the Convention on the Elimination of all forms of Discrimination Against Women (CEDAW) helps but the UK has no domestic delivery mechanism. Article 40 of the Istanbul Convention, 2012, which requires the UK to take action to eliminate sexual harassment and other violence against women as a form of discrimination and a human rights abuse, has been signed but not ratified in the UK (413). These agreements provide a bill of rights for women that should allow governments to be held to a set of standards. Equally, they are an instrument for lobbying states around their efforts to tackle male violence against women and girls, an aim which encompasses sexual harassment and abuse.

In the UK, there is the Equality Act 2010, which outlaws sexual harassment by service providers both in the public and private sector (37). The mechanisms of enforcement, through the Equality and Human Rights Commission (EHRC) and Government Equality Office (GEO) have been scrutinised by a parliamentary inquiry (they had their homework marked). The GEO was described as a small organisation that lacks power, moves around departments and lacks robust consultation with the voices of underfunded women's organisations (the main operators in this space) (418). The EHRC have been told they need to do more enforcement and publish data on this (137). They were seen to be missing a 'mandatory duty' to protect from harassment, supported by a code of practice around sexual harassment, in other words, the 'what and how' of enforcement. The inquiry looking at their work made a key point, it should not be left to individuals to police inequality on a case by case basis, a structural approach is much more effective (419). In other words, they could do better and should show their workings out.

Taking on board the inquiry finding, we need to frame this as 'collective failure' rather than a series of isolated incidents. International and domestic laws may signal intent and provide direction but most prevention work happens in workplaces, educational institutions and other specific 'settings' or structures, where bodies acting as accountable 'custodians' can be identified.

Telling people how to behave is not enough, settings need to take an holistic approach to modelling the change they are trying to achieve and make the business, moral and civil rights case for improvements (420).

> "If I don't say something then it's never going to end but then everyone has to say something."
>
> (230)

Everyone means men as well as women, as agents of change. If sexual bullying is an expression of male dominance then that is what you have to change to prevent it, not only structurally through diversity and equality but in who you teach young people to be.

PROTECT YOUR DAUGHTERS EDUCATE YOUR SONS

> "All too often I hear or read men saying 'Not all men are like that'.
> I acknowledge this, but these men need to play a more active role in preventing harassment by actively challenging the men who do behave in such a manner. When I was a child, why did none of the bystanders defend me? Even now as an adult, why has no man ever intervened to challenge the perpetrators regarding their behaviour?" (Woman 24–35, inquiry witness)
>
> (87)

International research across five countries has shown us how to do this: involve, encourage, and learn from those many men who do not use violence or sexual violence (421,422). Men and boys need to be able to call out the harassing behaviour of friends and tell them to stop but also earn 'man brownie points' for doing so (423). In looking at the purpose of performing manliness, we can understand that often the difficulty with 'being a real man' is other men. Sexual violence as an expression of one form of masculinity is a problem to us all.

> "I think men need to talk to each other and say actually, dude, don't do that, that's really messed up."
>
> (181)

Gender transformation work with males may be the best place to start addressing norms (424,425) with programmes such as Real Consent (426). The same norms that cause young men and their friends so much harm (290). It is important that this is done alongside structural, legal and societal level reform (390,427). The potential words to describe men's positive contribution to stopping harassment are many; agent, ally, bystander, champion, activist. Men's motives in engaging may well not be inequality or feminism, but with #MeToo, a recognition that this has and is happening to many women they know and love:

> "Over the past few months, I have been horrified by non-stop revelations about sex abuse by men. It's not just the grim details – it's the underlying truth that each new story drives home: that this is normal, and especially normal wherever men have power."
>
> (10)

There is up to date evidence around how to do this work (397), comprehensive overviews of what to do, what others do and what to expect in resistance, from academics such as Michael Flood (428) in Australia, the UK Government Equalities Office work by Stephen Burrell (429) and the American Psychological Association (APA) in the US (430). All start with the need to appeal to men rather than demonising them, acknowledging that there are a range of men as there are a range of women. Many resources highlight the harms connected to male domination through increased violence directed either outwards (at others) or inwards (towards the self through suicide) (270). These harms are compounded across the lifespan as self-worth is increasingly erased as aging men are less able to be the 'action hero' or become ill (but will not go to the doctor) (290). The author, Irving Welsh sums it up "the patriarchy's been fucking shit for men, too – they've been fucking blown to bits and shot at and they've worked in factories and mills and building sites and died young" (431).

For those on the up side of male dominance, doing something rather than nothing requires a motive, pointing to the gains of gender equality, and framing it as positive for all is a recommended starting point (432).

International agencies such as the WHO (397), the ICRW (417) and organisations like White Ribbon (433) Promundo and Plan International

(434) who promote healthy masculinity, suggest the following key features. Men should be given permission to feel a range of emotions, be encouraged to label them and express them, 'I am scared', 'I am sad'. They suggest discussion of what gender is and how stereotypes impact on everyone and how not being able to express sadness or shame turn into violence. Messages need to describe the difference between physical and mental strength of character, show what the 'man box' is, how it limits men and how it is healthy to step outside its rules. Encouraging critical conversations with other 'real men', talking about different ways of being and the acceptance of non–conformity all have a place. We need to celebrate masculine examples of empathy, humanity and caring as healthy and support men to be fathers (435). Men's positive contributions are often camouflaged and not spoken about, they need to be applauded as a means of giving permission to be caring. We need to translate that into behaviours that avoid punitive, parental discipline.

Long-term social norms work with men have demonstrated single study evidence of impact on later self-reported sexual aggression (436) and programmes focusing on male role models such as sporting coaches, e.g. 'Coaching Boys to Men', demonstrated an impact on wider violence (437). Providing the skills should also cover how to challenge inequality as individuals and from within organisations and how to visibly model the change (438). Intimate partner violence programmes such as 'Coaching Boys to Men' show that what is also needed is resistance to swopping one form of masculine dominance for another such as a 'white knight saves the oppressed' narrative. Finally, letting people know that sexual harassment, bullying and violence is about gender inequality, is key to them making the connections.

We will look at educational approaches for all young people later in this chapter but knowing they can be who they want in the world and giving them permission to step outside the prison of gender stereotypes is crucial for all. What happens when this message produces negative reactions? Tension and conflict are part of change and are to be expected and as far as possible, held and understood rather than avoided.

Holding resistance

How do you deal with resistance? By understanding it as a way of coping with threat. Who is threatened by what? Those advantaged by the current balance of power are likely to resist efforts to change that, so it comes mainly from men (439). What does it look like? Put simply: 'I don't'; '#Not all men'; in other words denial or disavowal (439). Analysis of reactions against #MeToo on Twitter came down to six basic ideas: invalidating claims, suggesting accusations were false or framing them as having alternative motives, prioritising harm to the accused, general concerns for male privilege and questioning the integrity of #MeToo as a whole (440). The great thing about the status quo is that one way to resist change is simply to do nothing, inaction can be effective. Placating or pretending to go along with messages that challenge male dominance, whilst undermining their meaning, has also been used to actively resist change (439).

Survey data on male students' reactions to a university-based program on sexual violence showed 32% thought it might be useful but 11% reacted angrily; "I would be outraged because it stereotypes men as the perpetrator" (441). Research on reactions to online campaigns have also found this spectrum of 'engaged to opposed' (442). That backlash is also often targeted against women who represent 'threat' in their intrusion into male spaces and spheres of influence such as female MPs (74) or leaders (443). Women human rights defenders face more threats of violence than their male counterparts, both because they are women and because they are challenging norms around gender, by participating in politics and the public sphere (444).

Given how much we already know about what resistance looks like, evidence-based responses can be prepared for (439). Teaching strategies need to balance the need to challenge but also to support. This requires the generation of safe spaces, true participation, and skilled professionals using a variety of approaches, within a whole organisation approach, enduring long enough to hold the backlash (438). Also, securing powerful stakeholders and role models buy in, targeting those most likely to resist and tying the work to goals of fairness and social justice have been shown to help.

De-escalating resistance can often be achieved by simply not 'blaming men' but focusing on what they lose out on, what they can gain, and supporting them with examples in finding other ways to be a man.

Let us leave behind the idea that men attack women and prevention is about telling women how to avoid it (318); social norms are the starting point for effective prevention and these can be taught.

TEACH IT – TACKLE THE CULTURE AND MAKE THE CONNECTIONS

People often arrive at sexual violence/abuse through relationships which have been mutually created and generally consensual until they are not (44). They bring with them a complexity of feelings and beliefs, derived from sex education, friends, family and the media as they attempt to claim what Hirsch and Khan call 'sexual citizenship'.

We know that comprehensive, age appropriate, inclusive sex and relationship education set within a frame of gender and intersectional inequality can work (425). We have known this for a long time and yet sex and relationship education in schools only became mandatory in the UK in 2020 with an expanded national framework (445).

School-based sex education can act as a vehicle for a range of gender transformative learning opportunities around healthy relationships, consent, bystander programmes, sexual harassment awareness, taking disclosure, etc. The evidence for schools points to the potential for group-based work and experts recommend starting young (58) through graduated programmes that scaffold the building blocks of consent and relationship negotiation in order to move to more mature issues of: healthy relationships; consent (446); sexual health and bystander intervention (447). This is not limited to just schools or school age individuals, 43% of young people reach Higher Education without having had sex and therefore continue to need and say they want, sex and relationship advice (448). Half have watched porn and a third currently do so (448), demonstrating that the gap will be filled from somewhere. Better somewhere that promotes healthy mutual relationships than routinely sexualising female subordination (328).

A gender and inequality lens can make programmes five times more powerful (425). Education on sexual harassment and violence cuts across issues of self-esteem, appearance, masculinity and inequality. In addition, a 2018 UK-wide consultation (445) captured the views of many expert bodies and individuals on the need to cover issues such as pornography as well as gender discrimination, racism, identity and harassment. At some point, within a developmentally paced programme, young people should be able to make the links between 'cat-calling' and more serious sexual assault and should be provided with the tools to critically understand the impact of aggressive pornography/sexting and the culture of online platforms, much of which is spelt out in the UK government's guidance (445). Consent and bystanders training are different doors onto a common set of topics and we have good review level evidence of what these should be.

The evidence base as a starting point means it should also be the end point. Schools should evaluate the impact of their work. How does young people's behaviour change and how can this be tied to the work done through 'a theory of change': why did A lead to B to result in C? What commonly used measures such as rape myth acceptance, can we use to show improvement and for how long does the change last, six months? One year?

For schools, this summary of the evidence draws on existing synthesis by Michael Flood (428), review studies (140,425); the Women and Equalities report on violence in schools (165); wider violence against women and girls evidence synthesis (449) as well as my own research in the field (307,333,450) and its application within a university setting (107,451,452).

Schools should embed sex and relationship education within a whole school approach that covers the topics throughout the curriculum, policy and practice, culture and environment. Good school-based sex education reaches out to consult parents, communities and local or national topic-based organisations. Why? Because it teaches the links between how we behave as individuals to each other and how institutions and organisations behave.

There is no need to start from scratch, work should be built on existing theory and evidence. Sounds obvious, but the teaching should be good quality with plenty of interaction and participation. There should be a focus on community, negotiating how to work together, and links to positive citizenship educational goals. Well evaluated, off-the-shelf teaching materials such as 'Safe Dates' (453) and 'Shifting Boundaries' (454) show real world behaviour change around thoughts and attitudes as well as skills and behaviour and can be starting points for consultative adaptation for local delivery. There are also well evaluated programmes on critical approaches to porn such as Maree Crabb's 'It's Time to Talk' from Australia (332).

Not surprisingly, standalone events/talks lack evidence of effect, so programmes should be cyclical, sustainable with messages mirrored throughout the organisation. Confusion over 'no meaning no' will not be cleared up in one lesson. Why, because it is not confusion around what no means but her 'no' not counting against his 'yes'. It is about whose account is credible and heard and whose is dismissed.

Resistance or backlash should be expected if work is effective in challenging behaviour and therefore, containing and dealing with it should be thought through. Staff need to be supported in how to handle disclosures of both victimisation and perpetration, through good training and guidance-based school policy and procedures (455,456) which are clear, timely, balanced and trauma informed. Staff live within the society whose social norms around gender drive sexual violence and therefore cannot be expected to address changing the culture without their own gender transformative training. Responding to someone telling you of sexual harassment and abuse is trauma informed when it starts from a point of belief, removes blame from the victim, listens to their experience and restores control over next steps as far as possible (once the limits of confidentiality have been shared), alongside information on the benefits of telling. Victim/survivors having to tell their story multiple times can be re-traumatising and short-cut access to early expert support should be an option. Schools have to sit within safeguarding regulations but consequences need to be case specific, informed by the wishes of the victim/survivor and range from internal measures to referral to statutory agencies. In general, there should be immediate and sustained removal of the person committing an act of perpetration from proximity to the victim/survivor. Early access to ongoing support should be in collaboration with local specialist sexual violence agencies.

Informed use of single sex/mixed groups, external agencies, peer educators, diverse representation of sexuality, male/female staff could build towards an environment that supports disclosure. The language and content of a whole organisation should not exclude people with protected characteristics and back this up by being seen to handle behaviour that excludes.

Triangulate the data: whole school/university programmes mean incidents are recorded through a range of reporting routes and monitored and scrutinised for patterns. What is in place for students should also be in place for staff in dealing with workplace sexual harassment (111).

Schools are not the only setting for this work and backing up messages from a range of sources works best and can include Public Health campaigns similar to the UK-based 'This is Abuse' information campaign (457). Beyond education, other settings based education can work, look at recent review evidence for work with juries around acceptance of rape myths (458)

Prevention is obviously the way forward but how do we expand beyond a criminal justice, reactive approach? By using a 'theory of change' lens we can unpick or understand the relative contribution of the courts which may still be useful in showing society where the boundaries lie. This is helpful but can only work if the law is applied, drafting laws and then not enforcing them may be more harmful.

MARK THE BOUNDARIES ACROSS STRUCTURES

Once prevention fails, enforcement needs to be used to show society where the boundaries lie (459). Currently, this does not happen enough and enforcement seems incomplete (see Chapter 6, Legal Immunity). Reporting is low and the commitment to culture change, patchy. In workplace harassment those already doing the work generally are the ones volunteering to be studied (460).

Higher Education has been the focus of much attention within efforts to research and prevent sexual bullying and to some extent provides a test ground for a settings approach. As the sector moves towards the recommended workplace 'statement of expectations' (138) which sets out details around how to handle reported cases (461), it is useful to compare the UK approach to sexual harassment/abuse in education with that of other countries. The UK frames abuse reports in Higher Education as 'service user complaints' but the US Title IX laws (115) treat it as a matter of civil rights, the right of women to get an education without systematic barriers. A civil rights-based approach gives recourse to a greater range of laws. A rights-based approach to sexual harassment and abuse in education is possible in the UK, through the Equality Act's public sector duty of care but such structural efforts remain untested (462).

Civil rights might be assumed as fundamental to the international aid sector, a setting in which problems of sexual abuse and exploitation have emerged (463) and where power differentials are a characteristic of their crisis response environment. The sector's response however, has been limited to better enforcement against individuals but less around structural prevention through changing power differentials and who gets the jobs (464). They have yet to establish a mechanism for collating the complaints that are made or analysing patterns across the sector. A review of the evidence around factors contributing to the sexual bullying and exploitation pointed to organisational social norms and cultures which supported hypermasculinity, tolerated harassment or framed it as 'banter' or 'jokes'. Failing to call out behaviour blocks the 'this is not okay' function of rebukes; contributes to staff homogeneity as those targeted more leave (108); produces poor safeguarding; and weakens management and their control systems (463).

The aid sector provides a case study (where research has been done) on certain places and spaces that intensify male entitlement (463) and other evidence points to male dominated workplaces such as Science, Technology, Engineering and Medicine (465) and the military (466,467).

Enforcing the legal boundaries can also extend to things like age verification of commercial online porn sites, controlling access to porn as well as teaching critical approaches to dealing with it. Pornography could be treated in the same way as online access to tobacco, alcohol, weapons and gambling; children cannot access them because of strict age controls (468). The UK was leading the way towards age verification but this may be side stepped in the current Online Harms bill (469). The proposed limit is just on 'user uploaded content', giving the large commercial sites such as Pornhub and xHamster an easy opt-out by simply removing it (469). However, boundaries are moving towards requiring more provider accountability for content through tech platforms used to view porn and card companies used to pay for it. Financial services have been focused by legal claims from those whose victimisation has been filmed, uploaded then sold and sold again (470) and they want to limit potential liability. Other recommendations include better recognition of the nature of online abuse such as image-based sexual abuse (53) and regulation of providers for the content they carry (79).

Changes to the law such as the introduction of hate crimes status for street sexual harassment, lack impact evidence but are potentially meaningful for clearer messaging about behavioural boundaries (10). In the same vein, public health campaigns across media and social media can address social norms (457) as well as face to face interventions designed to directly change those norms (436).

One impact of #MeToo was the shock some men expressed about how common the experience of sexual harassment is among the women they knew (10). Uncovering, recording, giving voice and space for testimony is a powerful tool that addresses the silence at the heart of many victims' trauma.

COUNT IT – TO MAKE IT COUNT

If we are to truly address sexual violence and abuse, we need to get better at counting it. The reporting gap explored in Chapter 6 requires us to do much more than tell people to report; we need to create disclosure supportive environments (307). Data also needs to be collected beyond the point of telling, to cover how it was handled and what happened as a result.

Prevention in organisations needs to include a range of ways in which to document the prevalence and patterns of sexual harassment/abuse (111). This can only be achieved by earning those reports from victim/survivors (471). Policy and procedures that describe how an organisation responds to a report should be subject to user (complainant and accused) evaluation and audited against key criteria of timeliness, transparency and balance (123).

Across a number of sectors, whilst researching this book, I have come across resistance to asking about sexual harassment for fear of 'being seen to have a problem'. There is no evidence for this assumption and likely the opposite is true (115). Reluctance to document or address sexual harassment lies in a perceived risk to reputation (115) and without mandatory standards from government such as annual anonymous prevalence surveys, it can be easily ignored. Data only exists in pockets such as Higher Education campus climate surveys, London transport research and some workplaces. Crime data does not do the job and victim/survivors have had to find their own ways of giving testimony (hence #MeToo). Activism has also filled that silence, for example, the Femicide Census (26) seeks to uncover the information gap around male violence against women and girls by publishing the rates of how many women are killed by men (472), information that is not otherwise available.

A range of social movements, led by victim/survivor voice, have emerged beyond #MeToo, including; Everyone's Invited (7); Hollaback (473); It's Not OK (474); Time's Up (475) and for child sexual abuse, I Will Be Heard (476). There is power in testimony: victims/survivors sharing their experiences has produced rapid (sometimes panicked) change (295). Reporting should be the norm, and mechanisms for reporting should not filter accounts, letting only stereotypical or 'serious' experiences through (477). For future prevention, those who do not wish to proceed to formal reporting need a way for their experiences to be collated and examined; anonymous online outlets have partly democratised testimony (478). Former UN executive, Purna Sen (479) reminds us that power stays with those who have a voice, against those who are assumed to be lying or who are not seen as credible. The same is true of how we see the costs to the perpetrator as greater than that of survivors. Hearing victim/survivor testimony may produce a much needed cultural shift in visibility and greater understanding of the life-long impact of experiencing sexual abuse/violence. How can we encourage and better value it?

MAKE TELLING EASIER

Asking can hurt but not telling can hurt more (480)

> "By the time I was 39 years old it'd become easier to talk about it.
> When I was younger, however, the words just wouldn't come out. It
> was like they were stuck in my throat and I couldn't breathe properly."
> Survivor
>
> (196)

Creating a safe space and 'earning' disclosure from survivors (307) demands that we adequately resource prevention and response work (123). Using the right language to signal that the response will be sensitively received and understood in a culturally competent manner is a start. What does that look like? At first glance, demonstrating diversity across responders, using labels that are inclusive and sensitive to sexuality, gender, race and avoiding rape myth based responses such as 'how much had you had to drink?' (298). Again, as part of a whole organisation approach, good staff training should focus on reducing distress, responding from a place of belief, explaining procedures and allowing victim/survivors to control as much as possible what happens next (123).

Existing guidance describes the powerful steps of trauma informed belief, listening, offering options and facilitating control over what happens next (123). Based on the accounts in my own research in which self-blame presented such a barrier to disclosure, I would expand the idea of blame to specifically 'un-blaming' the victim/survivor or emphasising that what has happened to them was not their fault (471).

We have seen how first reactions can dictate how able that person is to get the help they need and studies show that a range of services (especially in crisis frontline healthcare) could screen or ask more about sexual violence (298). From my own research with students answering anonymous survey questions, we evidenced about half had experienced sexual harassment and abuse in the last five years but of those subsequently seeking help at health services, only a small percentage (7 of 32) told that service what had happened to them. Prevalence of unacknowledged rape and difficulty clearly labelling those experiences requires a nuanced approach to enquiry (308). Current healthcare screening is often more focused on asking safeguarding questions (are you in imminent danger) or domestic violence questions (are you afraid of your partner), missing the many sexual assault/abuse experiences reported within shorter, 'dating' timelines and or using coercion (481).

The evidence base in sexual violence screening is difficult to use as it often conflates domestic or intimate partner violence with sexual violence (482,483) however, cues should be followed up by trained staff and simply routine universal asking may increase reporting (484). The dilemma remains one of taking a 'screening' approach and asking everyone or 'case finding' by asking those who show signs of having experienced sexual harassment/abuse. My own work with specialist sexual violence counselling services has shown that there is no evidence of one 'best way'. The goal of screening should also be considered. Referral to specialist services may feel like a good outcome for the professional but something as small as 'hearing well' or simply signposting for future disclosure may be enough for victim/survivors (485). Research around online safeguarding points to the need to emphasise what good may result from telling, including the benefits of specialist help (486). Positive examples of reporting are rare and it may be important for organisations to highlight an alternative narrative of good outcomes. The wording of any screening needs to be broad, such as 'has something sexual happened that you did not want or felt you could not say no to' or 'did you have any problems around consent'? Victim/survivor groups with whom I work suggest a less intrusive blanket statement given to all about where to get help. Good research evidence is needed on this.

Anonymous reporting and mapping could be useful to evidence prevalence, patterns and the impact of prevention work. For example, universities are increasingly introducing anonymous, online reporting systems such as Report and Support (81) and the Equalities and Human Rights Commission guidance recommends their introduction across workplaces (111). They offer a useful tool against which to assess impact, with increased reporting an indicator of success in creating a disclosure supportive environment (123).

A key part of the problem evidenced in my own work with survivors is finding the language that they feel reflects their own experience (307). The problem at the heart of the mismatch is society's obsession with 'textbook rape' something research has called 'tightrope talk' or negotiation of words and the blame they denote in the telling of sexual violence (351). As a result victims struggle with the weight and perceived meaning of the labels offered (487), sometimes preferring broader descriptors such as 'a problem with consent' (307). Only wider education around healthy relationships and greater recognition of the spectrum of abuse can address these barriers. Reporting should be flexible, model diversity and understand the internal struggle to 'name' the range of experiences from street-based, stranger intrusion to sexual assault by a friend or aquaintance.

The last ask on this list of needs is early access to specialist services (298). This requires there to be well funded and accessible specialist counselling available. In my own area, the waiting list to access sexual violence counselling is currently nine months. The local specialist Sexual Abuse Referral Centre (SARC) has had to repeatedly, competitively bid against their own charity partners to provide the same support they already deliver but for less money, an experience mirrored across the sector (488). Women's organisations are at the forefront of activism, reform and service provision; they should get stable and sustainable funding to meet increasing demand (489). If you are going to try and improve reporting, make sure the help is in place to hold the fall out of that. Spikes in demand for support often occur around highly visible cases or depictions of sexual violence in popular drama and point to the importance of what the media has to say about sexual violence both in news and entertainment (490).

CHANGE HOW YOU SHOW IT

The UK Advertising Standard Agency and the Committee on Advertising Practice have drawn a clear line under stopping sexualisation and objectification across our daily diet of advertising. Prompted by the evidence, they have acknowledged the real world harm of rigid gender stereotyping and the policing of this by the mocking of non-conformity (378). Their work points to a 'drip feed' accumulation of messaging over time from adverts that may seem unproblematic viewed in isolation. Much like the 'hand on the knee' (27) at work can be trivialised until put in the context of life-long, low level acts of sexual harassment that result in exclusion (233).

In drama, particularly crime drama, we have considered the increasingly graphic use of sexual violence as entertainment (491) and the inroads diversity is making (see Chapter 6). Research has shown more women in the writing rooms; creating the scripts can push back against problematic content. A pushback which sometimes wins praise (25%) but can also get you fired (10%) (492) and may not yet extend to age, ethnicity, sexuality or disability (492). There are also tools such as the Bechdel-Wallace test (493) in film which simply looks for scenes in which at least two women (with names) talk to each other about something other than men. Work from the Geena Davis Institute on Gender in Media also points to the need to show a range of masculinities, ('if he can see it he will be it') in children's programming (494). At its heart, a growth in diversity drives both the recognition of problematic stereotypes as well as the greater freedom to call it out.

The work of '#NO MORE RAPE MYTHS' in calling out news media coverage, highlights the use of narratives that demonise survivors and female sexual agency. The Independent Press Standard Organisation publishes guidance on reporting, but the focus is more on protecting victim/survivor anonymity. More comprehensive are #NO MORE RAPE MYTHS' own reporting standards that remind journalists:

• All articles dealing with sexual violence should include contact details for support organisations

- Headlines should not undermine, minimise or excuse the issue of sexual violence
- Coverage should use the correct terms for sexual violence, not 'sex' for rape or 'child porn' for child sexual abuse or 'revenge porn' for image-based sexual abuse
- Articles on sexual violence should not include or appear next to images or links which undermine this issue
- Online commentary should be turned off in order not to provide a platform for misogyny
- Finally, court cases should be covered in a balanced way between defendant and victim and overall reporting needs to avoid perpetuating rape myths (495).

USE THE RIGHT MAPS – LANGUAGE AND FRAMING

Incidents have meaning and should be read both as the experience of those involved but connected back to an expression of norms. The maps we use to understand sexual harassment/abuse need to cover both these points and all that falls in between (114). An 'ecological model' or map allows us to understand sexual bullying from the experience of the person, the social meaning of the behaviour as well as what shapes how their community makes sense of it. It also opens up the breadth of policy and environmental and public health prevention tools beyond traditional criminal justice beyond 'one penis at a time' (496) responses. Prevention programmes for all male violence against women (including sexual) such as RESPECT (390) address work across society, community, interpersonal and individual levels and demand an evidence-based approach to work using a clear theory of how change will happen. Societal or community level interventions such as grant funding and legislation to tackle male violence against women and girls have been directly linked to reductions in sexual offending rates (139,140). Work within prevalence hotspots such as the night time economy (497) and its currency of alcohol (498) also shows results. The lines we draw around the evidence, (domestic violence vs all violence vs sexual violence), are often blurred with sexual and domestic settings combined. They are heavily connected (48) but a domestic focus excludes much of the common acquaintance perpetration that victim/survivors would not identify, even under the wider title of intimate partner violence (499).

What we call it matters, how we label acts and individuals speaks directly to how we choose to understand. First person labelling in which we call out the person and not the act, has long been recognised as a problem by forensic psychologists (500). Why call someone what we do not want them to be? The work of Hirsh and Kahn put labelling the behaviour at the heart of their in-depth account of campus sexual assault focusing on acts of perpetration (44) and connected first person labelling to the minoritisation of other groups (501).

Defining a whole person by a behaviour or experience is called cognitive distortion (430). For those experiencing 'rape' or 'consent issues' the need to move on from the victim identity has already been acknowledged in the adoption of the term victim/survivor (487).

> "I don't wanna be denoted as a victim for the fucking rest of my life –
> 'cause that's hard to live down as well, like you're a victim, how do
> you get on from that? Like it's tough, you have to do really well to get
> beyond the label of a victim." Imogen

(487)

In the same way using terms such as 'experiencing sexual violence', 'acts of perpetration' or 'people who have carried out sexual offences' is a person-first approach which may provide a way of moving forward (376).

In summary,

- Prevention should have a strategy based on theory and the right maps
- Prevention should be gender and inequality centred
- Don't just talk diversity, model it
- Educate and recruit male allies
- Teach it and mark the boundaries
- 'Earn' reporting and consistently respond with trauma informed processes and enforcement
- Join up across landscapes (settings, policy, healthcare, criminal justice)
- Count it and show the impact in how we retell it
- Join up national and international work
- Be in for the long haul

If nothing else, use the evidence and be led by the experts who are the victims/survivors, those who work with them and the academics who do the research.

Conclusions

This book has necessarily focused on sex within sexual violence, but at the same time, issues of sexual abuse and harassment seem only to be clothed in the words and acts of bad sex. We know sexual violence is less about sex and desire and more about the eroticisation of sexual bullying. Sexual citizenship (44) should be facilitated by good communication to strengthen intimacy and the rights and responsibilities of all parties including the uncoerced right to say no (445). Like a good conversation, healthy relationships require listening, mutuality and understanding.

I have sat through formal proceedings in which a survivor shared their experience of being sexually assaulted whilst too drunk to consent. The accused provided an account of wronged innocence and projected motives of regretted consensual sex. The hardest part was listening to the reactions of those there to adjudicate. They believed her but her account just did not seem to matter as much as his or what might happen to him. It was like her volume was turned down; was I listening in a different way, was I hearing something different?

So much of this book is underlined by the lack of words and spaces for survivors, silence fed on shame and nowhere to tell. Our society is very bad at giving young people support in developing the language of open communication to negotiate healthy relationships but also how to protect themselves from unhealthy ones through recognising abuse or standing up for their own bodily autonomy (445). The only way back from this is through communication and listening to victim/survivors taking back their voice, visibility and themselves and demanding that all those 'men who don't' raise their voices alongside women activists.

Sexual consent is both verbal and not verbal and requires sensitive mutual negotiation and ongoing checking out of what is okay. In stereotypical terms, men and women have been taught different meanings for key signals; 'moving a hand away' to a woman may clearly say no thank you,

DOI: 10.4324/9781003168591-9

yet her male partner might understand 'ask again in a minute' (372). At the same time, how she is situated (gender, race, ability, sexual orientation) can turn down her volume, her 'no' is less audible and her account less credible.

Sexual bullying is complex, encompassing the political, legal, social and health fields but that messiness does not stop us seeing where the harm is greatest and what the evidence tells us we must do to try stop it. Progress is not regular, the combination of greater recognition of the dangers for women in #MeToo has also come at the same time as the near normalisation of the aggressive pornography that contributes to their victimisation. If writing this book has taught me anything, it is that not only can we change this but that we must and that we already know how. A last word has to go to a survivor

> "So it's been harrowing . . . it felt easier to bury it and move on but the #MeToo movement. Well its really shocking isn't it, you know, the re-education of society."

(240)

References

1. Horvath MA, Alys L, Massey K, Pina A, Scally M, Adler JR. Basically. . . *Porn is Everywhere: A Rapid Evidence Assessment on the Effects That Access and Exposure to Pornography Has on Children and Young People*. Office of the Children's Commissioner for England; 2013.

2. @the_T_inHistory. I knew him. He was my best friend's cousin. I didn't know any better and it wasn't the first time he assaulted me. Have I told anyone this until now? No! Why? Because I knew no one would believe me. #MeToo [Internet]. @the_T_inHistory. 2018 [cited 2021 Sep 14]. Available from: https://twitter.com/the_T_inHistory/status/1045125264802484225.

3. Modrek S, Chakalov B. The #MeToo movement in the United States: Text analysis of early twitter conversations. *J Med Internet Res* [Internet]. 2019 Sep 3 [cited 2021 Feb 5];21(9). Available from: www.ncbi.nlm.nih.gov/pmc/articles/PMC6751092/.

4. Loney-Howes R, Mendes K, Romero DF, Fileborn B, Puente SN. Digital footprints of #MeToo. *Fem Media Stud*. 2021 Feb 11:1–18.

5. Manne K. *Down Girl: The Logic of Misogyny*. Oxford University Press; 2017.

6. Jayanetti C. New equalities commissioner attacked 'modern feminism' and #MeToo. *The Guardian* [Internet]. 2020 Nov 22 [cited 2021 May 27]. Available from: www.theguardian.com/society/2020/nov/22/new-equalities-commissioner-attacked-modern-feminism-and-metoo.

7. Everyone's invited [Internet]. Everyone's invited. 2021 [cited 2021 May 13]. Available from: www.everyonesinvited.uk.

8. Mullany L, Trickett L. Misogyny hate crime evaluation report [Internet]. 2018. Available from: www.nottingham.ac.uk/lipp/documents/misogyny-evaluation-report.pdf.

9. APPG. The prevalence and reporting of sexual harassment in UK public spaces: A report by the APPG for UN women [Internet]. 2021. Available from: www.unwomenuk.org/site/wp-content/uploads/2021/03/APPG-UN-Women-Sexual-Harassment-Report_Updated.pdf.

10. Reed D. Consent is an insufficient ethic for sex [Internet]. *Medium*. 2018 [cited 2021 May 20]. Available from: https://ddotreed.medium.com/consent-is-a-necessary-but-insufficient-ethic-for-sex-a9451d52e9bf.

11. Member of the public. Street harassment of women and girls in public places inquiry (SPP0064) [Internet]. 2018 [cited 2021 Feb 12]. Available from: http://data.parliament.uk/WrittenEvidence/CommitteeEvidence.svc/EvidenceDocument/Women%20

and%20Equalities/Sexual%20harassment%20of%20women%20and%20girls%20in%20 public%20places/written/79608.html.

12. Elkin M. *Sexual Offending: Victimisation and the Path Through the Criminal Justice System* [Internet]. Office for National Statistics; 2018. Available from: www.ons.gov.uk/peoplepopulationandcommunity/crimeandjustice/articles/ sexualoffendingvictimisationandthepaththroughthecriminaljusticesystem/2018-12-13.

13. Heck SE. From Anita Hill to Christine Blasey ford: A reflection on lessons learned | emerald insight. *Equal Divers Incl.* 2019;39(1):101–8.

14. Blasey Ford C. Written testimony of Dr. Christine Blasey ford [Internet]. 2018 [cited 2021 Sep 16]. Available from: www.judiciary.senate.gov/imo/media/doc/09-27-18%20Ford%20Testimony%20Updated.pdf.

15. Action aid. Fearless: Women's rights organisations key to ending violence against women and girls in our rapidly urbanising world [Internet]. 2016. Available from: www.actionaid.org.uk/sites/default/files/publications/safe_cities_for_women_ may_2016.pdf.

16. Kearl H, Johns NE, Raj A. Measuring #MeToo: A national study on sexual harassment and assault [Internet]. 2019 [cited 2020 Dec 17]. Available from: https:// stopstreetharassment.org/wp-content/uploads/2012/08/2019-MeToo-National-Sexual-Harassment-and-Assault-Report.pdf.

17. Lenton R, Smith MD, Fox J, Morra N. Sexual harassment in public places: Experiences of Canadian women. *Can Rev Sociol Can Sociol.* 1999;36(4):517–40.

18. Qaane E. *Harassment of Women in Afghanistan: A Hidden Phenomenon Addressed in Too Many Laws* [Internet]. Afghanistan Analysis Network; 2017. p. 9. Available from: www.afghanistan-analysts.org/en/reports/rights-freedom/harassment-of-women-in-afghanistan-a-hidden-phenomenon-addressed-in-too-many-laws/.

19. Rasha H, Shoukry A, Komsan NA. *'Clouds in Egypt's Sky' Sexual Harassment: From Verbal Harassment to Rape* [Internet]. ECRW; 2008. Available from: www.endvawnow. org/uploads/browser/files/ecrw_sexual_harassment_study_english.pdf.pdf.

20. Khan S, Greene J, Mellins CA, Hirsch JS. The social organization of sexual assault. *Annu Rev Criminol.* 2020;3(1):139–63.

21. World health organization. Global and regional estimates of violence against women: Prevalence and health effects of intimate partner violence and non-partner sexual violence [Internet]. 2013 [cited 2020 Dec 10]. Available from: www.who.int/ publications-detail-redirect/9789241564625.

22. Kelly L. The continuum of sexual violence. In: Hanmer J, Maynard M, editors. *Women, Violence and Social Control* [Internet]. London: Palgrave Macmillan UK; 1987 [cited 2021 May 27]. p. 46–60 (Explorations in Sociology). Available from: https:// doi.org/10.1007/978-1-349-18592-4_4.

23. Southgate J, Russell L. *Street Harassment It's not Ok: Girls Experiences and Views* [Internet]. Plan International UK; 2018. Available from: https://plan-uk.org/sites/default/ files/Documents/Policy/Reports%20and%20Briefs/plan-uk-street-harassment-report.pdf.

24. Women and equalities committee, house of commons. Sexual harassment of women and girls in public places [Internet]. 2018 Oct [cited 2021 Feb 12]. Available from: https:// publications.parliament.uk/pa/cm201719/cmselect/cmwomeq/701/70102.htm.

25. Ingala Smith K. Can you give me a link to 'counting dead men'? [Internet]. *Karen Ingala Smith.* 2014 [cited 2021 Jan 22]. Available from: https://kareningalasmith. com/2014/04/14/can-you-give-me-a-link-to-counting-dead-men/.

26. Femicide census [Internet] [cited 2021 Mar 11]. Available from: www.femicidecensus. org/.

27. Childs S. A hand on the knee, and other parliamentary problems. . . . *IPPR Prog Rev.* 2018;24(4):314–22.

28. Muehlenhard CL, Powch IG, Phelps JL, Giusti LM. Definitions of rape: Scientific and political implications. *J Soc Issues.* 1992;48(1):23–44.

29. Member of the public. Street harassment of women and girls in public places inquiry (SPP0030) [Internet]. 2018 [cited 2020 Dec 17]. Available from: http:// data.parliament.uk/WrittenEvidence/CommitteeEvidence.svc/EvidenceDocument/ Women%20and%20Equalities/Sexual%20harassment%20of%20women%20and%20 girls%20in%20public%20places/written/77566.html.

30. Coy M, Kelly L, Elvines F, Garner M, Kanyeredzi A. *Sex Without Consent, I Suppose That Is Rape": How Young People in England Understand Sexual Consent.* Office of the Children's Commissioner; 2013.

31. Vera-Gray F. Men's stranger intrusions: Rethinking street harassment. *Womens Stud Int Forum.* 2016;58:9–17.

32. Member of the public. Street harassment of women and girls in public places inquiry (SPP0019) [Internet]. 2018 [cited 2020 Dec 17]. Available from: http:// data.parliament.uk/WrittenEvidence/CommitteeEvidence.svc/EvidenceDocument/ Women%20and%20Equalities/Sexual%20harassment%20of%20women%20and%20 girls%20in%20public%20places/written/76945.html.

33. Phillips D, Curtice J, Phillips M, Perry J. National centre for social research (Great Britain). *British Social Attitudes.* 2018;35.

34. Lowe P. Street harassment of women and girls in public spaces inquiry (SPP0060) [Internet]. 2018 [cited 2021 Mar 5]. Available from: http://data.parliament.uk/Written Evidence/CommitteeEvidence.svc/EvidenceDocument/Women%20and%20Equal ities/Sexual%20harassment%20of%20women%20and%20girls%20in%20public%20 places/written/79599.html.

35. Betts L, Harding R, Peart S, Sjolin Knight C, Wright D, Newbold K. Adolescents' experiences of street harassment: Creating a typology and assessing the emotional impact. *J Aggress Confl Peace Res.* 2018 Jan 1;11(1):38–46.

36. Member of the public. Street harassment of women and girls in public places inquiry (SP0010) [Internet]. 2018 [cited 2021 Jan 5]. Available from: http://data.parliament. uk/WrittenEvidence/CommitteeEvidence.svc/EvidenceDocument/Women%20 and%20Equalities/Sexual%20harassment%20of%20women%20and%20girls%20 in%20public%20places/written/76844.html.

37. UK Parliament. *Equality Act* [Internet]. Statute Law Database; 2010. Available from: www.legislation.gov.uk/ukpga/2010/15/contents.

38. Scott K. Tackling sexual harassment at work when you don't want to report it – ABC everyday [Internet]. 2018 [cited 2021 Sep 10]. Available from: www.abc.net.au/ everyday/tackling-workplace-sexual-harassment-without-a-complaint/10500470.

39. Macpherson W. *The Stephen Lawrence Inquiry* [Internet]. Parliament; 1999 Feb. Available from: https://assets.publishing.service.gov.uk/government/uploads/system/uploads/ attachment_data/file/277111/4262.pdf.

40. Fielding L, Tzani-Pepelasi C, Ioannou M, Artinopoulou V. Sexual harassment on pub-lic transport in England: Prevalence, experiences and barriers to reporting. *Assess Dev Matters* [Internet]. 2021 Mar 23 [cited 2021 Oct 1]. Available from: https://shop.bps. org.uk/publications/Periodicals-by-Series/Assessment-and-Development-Matters.

41. Nottinghamshire Police. Street harassment of women and girls in public places inquiry (SPP0049) [Internet]. 2018 [cited 2021 Jan 5]. Available from: http://data.parliament. uk/WrittenEvidence/CommitteeEvidence.svc/EvidenceDocument/Women%20 and%20Equalities/Sexual%20harassment%20of%20women%20and%20girls%20 in%20public%20places/written/79374.html.

42. Page T, Bull A, Chapman E. Making power visible: 'Slow activism' to address staff sexual misconduct. *Violence Women*. 2019;25(11):1309–30.

43. BBC. How NOT to sexually harass someone | The Mash Report – BBC [Internet]. 2018 [cited 2021 Jan 5]. Available from: www.youtube.com/watch?v=TMfStd-3v330&feature=youtu.be.

44. Hirsch JS, Khan S. *Sexual Citizens: A Landmark Study of Sex, Power, and Assault on Campus*. WW Norton & Company; 2020.

45. Coy M, Garner M. Definitions, discourses and dilemmas: Policy and academic engagement with the sexualisation of popular culture. *Gend Educ*. 2012;24(3):285–301.

46. Fileborn B, O'Neill T. From "ghettoization" to a field of its own: A comprehensive review of street harassment research. *Trauma Violence Abuse* [Internet]. 2021 Jun [cited 2021 Jun 21]. Available from: https://journals.sagepub.com/doi/abs/10.1177/15248380211021608.

47. Papendick M, Bohner G. 'Passive victim – strong survivor'? Perceived meaning of labels applied to women who were raped. *PLoS One*. 2017 May 11;12(5):e0177550.

48. Kelly L. *Surviving Sexual Violence*. Wiley; 1988.

49. Transport for London. Street harassment of women and girls in public places inquiry (SPP0092) [Internet]. 2018 [cited 2021 Jan 7]. Available from: http://data.parliament. uk/WrittenEvidence/CommitteeEvidence.svc/EvidenceDocument/Women%20 and%20Equalities/Sexual%20harassment%20of%20women%20and%20girls%20 in%20public%20places/written/80885.html.

50. YouGov. Sexual harassment in the capital [Internet]. 2012 [cited 2021 Jan 7]. Available from: https://yougov.co.uk/topics/politics/articles-reports/2012/05/25/sexual-harassment-capital.

51. Gekoski A, Gray JM, Adler JR, Horvath MA. The prevalence and nature of sexual harassment and assault against women and girls on public transport: An international review. *J Criminol Res Policy Pract*. 2017;3(1):3–16.

52. British transport. Street harassment of women and girls in public places inquiry (SPP0110) [Internet]. 2018. Available from: http://data.parliament.uk/ WrittenEvidence/CommitteeEvidence.svc/EvidenceDocument/Women%20 and%20Equalities/Sexual%20harassment%20of%20women%20and%20girls%20 in%20public%20places/written/86159.html.

53. McGlynn C, Rackley E, Houghton R. Beyond 'revenge porn': The continuum of image-based sexual abuse. *Fem Leg Stud*. 2017;25(1):25–46.

54. Crown prosecution service. Voyeurism | The crown prosecution service. In: *The Code for Crown Prosecutors* [Internet]. 2019 [cited 2021 Sep 15]. Available from: www.cps. gov.uk/legal-guidance/voyeurism.

55. DI Cooper A. Sexual harassment of women and girls in public places inquiry (HC701) [Internet]. 2018 [cited 2021 Sep 15]. Available from: http://data.parliament.uk/written evidence/committeeevidence.svc/evidencedocument/women-and-equalities-com mittee/sexual-harassment-of-women-and-girls-in-public-places/oral/86061.html.

56. McGlynn C. Watching porn in public – a modern form of street harassment? [Internet]. *HuffPost UK*. 2017 [cited 2021 Sep 15]. Available from: www.huffingtonpost. co.uk/clare-mcglynn/watching-porn-in-public-a_2_b_14268708.html.

57. Daskalopoulou A, Zanette MC. Women's consumption of pornography: Pleasure, contestation, and empowerment. *Sociology*. 2020 Oct 1;54(5):969–86.

58. Sundaram V. Street harassment of women and girls in public places inquiry (SPP0059) [Internet]. 2018 [cited 2021 Jan 7]. Available from: http://data.parliament.uk/ WrittenEvidence/CommitteeEvidence.svc/EvidenceDocument/Women%20 and%20Equalities/Sexual%20harassment%20of%20women%20and%20girls%20 in%20public%20places/written/79597.html.

59. Drinkaware. Street harassment of women and girls in public places inquiry (SPP050) [Internet]. 2018. Available from: http://data.parliament.uk/WrittenEvidence/ CommitteeEvidence.svc/EvidenceDocument/Women%20and%20Equalities/ Sexual%20harassment%20of%20women%20and%20girls%20in%20public%20places/ written/79416.html.

60. Member of the public. Street harassment of women and girls in public places inquiry (SPP0082) [Internet]. 2018 [cited 2021 Jan 8]. Available from: http://data.parliament. uk/WrittenEvidence/CommitteeEvidence.svc/EvidenceDocument/Women%20 and%20Equalities/Sexual%20harassment%20of%20women%20and%20girls%20 in%20public%20places/written/79689.html.

61. Cowburn M. Invisible men: Social reactions to male sexual coercion – bringing men and masculinities into community safety and public policy. *Crit Soc Policy*. 2010 May 1;30(2):225–44.

62. Young women's trust. Street harassment of women in girls in public places inquiry (SP00075) [Internet]. 2018 [cited 2021 Jan 8]. Available from: http://data.parliament. uk/WrittenEvidence/CommitteeEvidence.svc/EvidenceDocument/Women%20 and%20Equalities/Sexual%20harassment%20of%20women%20and%20girls%20 in%20public%20places/written/79655.html.

63. Fedina L, Holmes JL, Backes BL. Campus sexual assault: A systematic review of prevalence research from 2000 to 2015. *Trauma Violence Abuse*. 2018;19(1):76–93.

64. Brecklin LR, Ullman SE. The roles of victim and offender alcohol use in sexual assaults: Results from the national violence against women survey. *J Stud Alcohol*. 2002;63(1):57–63.

65. Melkonian AJ, Ham LS. The effects of alcohol intoxication on young adult women's identification of risk for sexual assault: A systematic review. *Psychol Addict Behav*. 2018;32(2):162.

66. Persson S, Dhingra K. Attributions of blame in stranger and acquaintance rape: A multilevel meta-analysis and systematic review. *Trauma Violence Abuse*. 2020 Dec 7;1524838020977146.

67. Ingber S. #ThisIsNotConsent: Protests in Ireland after thong underwear cited in rape trial. *NPR* [Internet]. 2018 Nov 16 [cited 2021 Sep 16]. Available from: www.npr. org/2018/11/16/668636051/-thisisnotconsent-protests-in-ireland-after-thong-un derwear-cited-in-rape-trial.

68. Graham K, Bernards S, Wayne Osgood D, Abbey A, Parks M, Flynn A, et al. "Blurred lines?" Sexual aggression and barroom culture. *Alcohol Clin Exp Res*. 2014;38(5):1416–24.

69. Hohl K, Stanko EA. Complaints of rape and the criminal justice system: Fresh evidence on the attrition problem in England and Wales. *Eur J Criminol*. 2015;12(3):324–41.

70. Girlguiding. Girls' attitudes survey [Internet]. 2016. Available from: www.girlguiding. org.uk/globalassets/docs-and-resources/research-and-campaigns/girls-attitudes- survey-2016.pdf.

71. Girlguiding. Girls' Attitudes Survey: A snapshot of girls' and young womens lives. [Internet]. 2020. Available from: www.girlguiding.org.uk/globalassets/docs-and-resources/research-and-campaigns/girls-attitudes-survey-2020.pdf.

72. European women's lobby. #HerNetHerRights resource pack on ending online violence against women & girls in Europe [Internet]. 2017. Available from: www.womenlobby.org/IMG/pdf/hernetherrights_resource_pack_2017_web_version.pdf.

73. Ringrose J, Gill R, Livingstone S, Harvey L. *A Qualitative Study of Children, Young People and 'Sexting': A Report Prepared for the NSPCC* [Internet]. London, UK: NSPCC; 2012 May [cited 2021 Jan 8]. Available from: www.nspcc.org.uk/.

74. Insights AG. Unsocial media: Tracking twitter abuse against women MPs [Internet]. *Medium.* 2017 [cited 2021 Jan 8]. Available from: https://medium.com/@Amnesty Insights/unsocial-media-tracking-twitter-abuse-against-women-mps-fc28aeca498a.

75. Blum RW, Mmari K, Moreau C. It begins at 10: How gender expectations shape early adolescence around the world. *J Adolesc Health.* 2017;61(4):S3–S4.

76. Home affairs committee. Abuse, hate and extremism online inquiry (HC 609) [Internet]. 2017 [cited 2021 Jan 8]. Report No.: HC 609. Available from: www.equallyours.org.uk/inquiry-into-hate-crime-and-its-violent-consequences/.

77. Fawcett society, local government commission, local government information unit. Does local government work for women? Final report of the local government commission' [Internet]. 2017. Available from: www.fawcettsociety.org.uk/Handlers/Download.ashx?IDMF=0de4f7f0-d1a0-4e63-94c7-5e69081caa5f.

78. Holland KJ, Cortina LM, Magley VJ, Baker AL, Benya FF. Don't let COVID-19 disrupt campus climate surveys of sexual harassment. *Proc Natl Acad Sci.* 2020 Oct 6;117(40):24606–8.

79. EVAW alliance. VAWG principles for the online saftey bill 2021 [Internet]. 2021 [cited 2021 Sep 21]. Available from: www.endviolenceagainstwomen.org.uk/wp-content/uploads/VAWG-Principles-for-the-Online-Safety-Bill-150921.pdf.

80. Refuge. The naked threat: It's time to change the law to protect survivors from image-based abuse [Internet]. 2020. Available from: www.refuge.org.uk/wp-content/uploads/2020/07/The-Naked-Threat-Report.pdf.

81. Culture shift. Reporting workplace harassment with an anonymous reporting tool [Internet]. *Culture Shift* [cited 2021 May 21]. Available from: www.culture-shift.co.uk/.

82. Fenton R, Mott H, McCartan K, Rumney P. *A Review of Evidence for Bystander Intervention to Prevent Sexual and Domestic Violence in Universities* [Internet]. University of the West of England; 2016. Report No.: Centre for Legal Research: Working paper 6. Available from: https://assets.publishing.service.gov.uk/government/uploads/system/uploads/attachment_data/file/515634/Evidence_review_bystander_intervention_to_prevent_sexual_and_domestic_violence_in_universities_11April2016.pdf.

83. Latane B, Darley JM. Group inhibition of bystander intervention in emergencies. *J Pers Soc Psychol.* 1968;10(3):215.

84. Livingstone B, Wagner KC, Diaz ST, Liu A. *The Experience of Being Targets of Street Harassment in NYC: Preliminary Findings from a Qualitaitve Study of a Sample of 223 Voices Who Hollaback!* [Internet]. The Worker Institue at Cornell; 2012. Available from: www.ihollaback.org/fact-sheet-the-experience-of-being-targets-of-street-harassment-in-nyc/.

85. Southgate J, Russell L. Street harassment: It's not OK [Internet]. 2018 [cited 2020 Dec 10]. Available from: https://plan-uk.org/street-harassment/its-not-ok.

86. Vizvary M. *The Statement of Street Harassment in DC: A Report on the First Year of Implementing the Street Harassment Prevention Act* [Internet]. DC Office of Human Rights;

2020. Available from: https://ohr.dc.gov/sites/default/files/dc/sites/ohr/publication/attachments/OHR_SHPA_Report_APRIL2020_FINAL.pdf.

87. Member of the public. Street harassment of women and girls in public places inquiry (SP0064) [Internet]. 2018 [cited 2020 Dec 10]. Available from: http://data.parliament.uk/WrittenEvidence/CommitteeEvidence.svc/EvidenceDocument/Women%20and%20Equalities/Sexual%20harassment%20of%20women%20and%20girls%20in%20public%20places/written/79608.html.

88. Hamby S, Weber MC, Grych J, Banyard V. What difference do bystanders make? The association of bystander involvement with victim outcomes in a community sample. *Psychol Violence*. 2016;6(1):91–102.

89. Fileborn B. Bystander intervention from the victims' perspective: Experiences, impacts and justice needs of street harassment victims. *J Gend-Based Violence*. 2017;1(2):187–204.

90. Bows H, Fileborn B. Space, place and GBV. *J Gend-Based Violence*. 2020 Oct 1;4(3):299–307.

91. Zugelder MT. The consequences of #MeToo: Intended and not. What employers should do. *J Leadersh Account* [Internet]. 2019 [cited 2021 Sep 16];16(3). Available from: https://web.a.ebscohost.com/abstract?direct=true&profile=ehost&scope=site&authtype=crawler&jrnl=19138059&AN=137898970&h=Z32wvyUfUmeQEiAnY8q0VeWvsMJDs6uIq4A%2bcLWLjBfOBhhMeKkCj8C6StWDaeAMPSlR4qiN%2f%2fMelDB3VmX%2fCw%3d%3d&crl=c&resultNs=AdminWebAuth&resultLocal=ErrCrlNotAuth&crlhashurl=login.aspx%3fdirect%3dtrue%26profile%3dehost%26scope%3dsite%26authtype%3dcrawler%26jrnl%3d19138059%26AN%3d137898970.

92. ComRes. BBC – Sexual harassment in the workplace [Internet]. 2017 [cited 2021 Jan 8]. Available from: https://comresglobal.com/wp-content/uploads/2017/12/BBC-sexual-harassment_FINAL_v3.pdf.

93. Mayer M, Mott H, Henderson A, Marren C, Bazeley A. Tackling sexual harassment in the workplace report on employer actions to prevent and respond to workplace sexual harassment [Internet]. 2020. Available from: www.fawcettsociety.org.uk/Handlers/Download.ashx?IDMF=8eabc7f1-07c0-4d7e-9206-de431524301e.

94. 38 Degrees. Sexual harassment in the workplace inquiry (SHW0025) [Internet]. 2018 [cited 2021 Jan 8]. Available from: http://data.parliament.uk/writtenevidence/committeeevidence.svc/evidencedocument/women-and-equalities-committee/sexual-harassment-in-the-workplace/written/80195.pdf.

95. Nawrockyi K. Sexual harassment in the workplace inquiry (HC 725) [Internet]. 2018 [cited 2020 Dec 15]. Available from: http://data.parliament.uk/writtenevidence/committeeevidence.svc/evidencedocument/women-and-equalities-committee/sexual-harassment-in-the-workplace/oral/83116.html.

96. Feldblum CR, Lipnic VA. *Select Task Force on the Study of Harassment in the Workplace | U.S. Equal Employment Opportunity Commission* [Internet]. U.S Equal Employment Opportunity Commission; 2016 Jun [cited 2021 Jan 8]. Available from: www.eeoc.gov/select-task-force-study-harassment-workplace.

97. Women and equalities committee, house of commons. *Sexual Harassment in the Workplace* [Internet]. House of Commons; 2018 Jul p. 61. Available from: https://publications.parliament.uk/pa/cm201719/cmselect/cmwomeq/725/725.pdf.

98. Savanta:ComRes. Young women's trust – survey of MPs [Internet]. 2018 [cited 2021 Jan 8]. Available from: https://2sjjwunnql41ia7ki31qqub1-wpengine.netdna-ssl.com/wp-content/uploads/2018/03/YWT_MPs-Data-Tables_for-upload.pdf.

99. TUC. Sexual harassment of disabled women in the workplace: A TUC report [Internet]. 2021. Available from: www.fawcettsociety.org.uk/Handlers/Download.ashx?IDMF=8eabc7f1-07c0-4d7e-9206-de431524301e.

100. TUC. Sexual harassment of LGBT people in the workplace [Internet]. 2019 May [cited 2021 Jan 22]. Available from: www.tuc.org.uk/sites/default/files/LGBT_Sexual_Harassment_Report_0.pdf.

101. Government equalities office. 2020 sexual harassment survey [Internet]. 2020. Available from: https://assets.publishing.service.gov.uk/government/uploads/system/uploads/attachment_data/file/1002873/2021-07-12_Sexual_Harassment_Report_FINAL.pdf.

102. TUC. Still just a bit of banter? Sexual harassment in the workplace in 2016 [Internet]. 2016. Available from: www.cwu.org/wp-content/uploads/2017/11/EC11-3-Attachment-Sexual-harassment-in-the-workplace.pdf.

103. FLEX focus on labour exploitation (SHW0016). Sexual harassment in the workplace inquiry (SHW0016) [Internet]. 2018. Available from: http://data.parliament.uk/writtenevidence/committeeevidence.svc/evidencedocument/women-and-equalities-committee/sexual-harassment-in-the-workplace/written/80111.pdf.

104. UNISON. Sexual harassment is a workplace issue guidance and model policy [Internet]. 2020. Available from: www.unison.org.uk/content/uploads/2020/02/25965-1.pdf.

105. Blackburn J. Sexual harassment in the workplace inquiry (HC 725) [Internet]. 2018. Available from: http://data.parliament.uk/writtenevidence/committeeevidence.svc/evidencedocument/women-and-equalities-committee/sexual-harassment-in-the-workplace/oral/84706.pdf.

106. TUC. Sexual harassment in the workplace inquiry (SHW0031) [Internet]. 2018. Available from: http://data.parliament.uk/WrittenEvidence/CommitteeEvidence.svc/EvidenceDocument/Women%20and%20Equalities/Sexual%20harassment%20in%20the%20workplace/written/80264.html.

107. McCartan K, Meyrick J, Thomas Z, Kowalska A. *Understanding and Responding to Sexual Violence at UWE.* Internal report University of the West of England; 2019.

108. Blackstone A, Uggen C, McLaughlin H. The economic and career effects of sexual harassment on working women. *Gend Soc.* 2017;31(3):333–58.

109. Percival T, Gibbons L. Beyond #MeToo: Addressing workplace sexual misconduct cases and the targeted use of non-disclosure agreements. *Brigh Young Univ Prelaw Rev* [Internet]. 2021 Apr 1;35(1). Available from: https://scholarsarchive.byu.edu/byuplr/vol35/iss1/9.

110. McLaughlin H, Uggen C, Blackstone A. Sexual harassment, workplace authority, and the paradox of power. *Am Sociol Rev.* 2012;77(4):625–47.

111. EHRC. Sexual harassment and harassment at work: Technical guidance | [Internet]. 2020 [cited 2021 May 21]. Available from: www.equalityhumanrights.com/en/publication-download/sexual-harassment-and-harassment-work-technical-guidance.

112. Hersch J. Sexual harassment in the workplace. *IZA World Labor* [Internet]. 2015 Oct 1 [cited 2021 Sep 16]. Available from: https://wol.iza.org/articles/sexual-harassment-in-workplace/long.

113. Crebbin W, Campbell G, Hillis DA, Watters DA. Prevalence of bullying, discrimination and sexual harassment in surgery in Australasia. *ANZ J Surg.* 2015;85(12):905–9.

114. Hagemann-White C, Kavemann B, Kindler H, Meysen T, Puchert R, Busche M, et al. *Factors at Play in the Perpetration of Violence Against Women, Violence Against Children and Sexual Orientation Violence-a Multi-Level Interactive Model* [Internet]. European Commission; 2010. Available from: www.humanconsultancy.com/assets/understanding-perpetration/understanding-perpetration.html.

115. Towl GJ, Walker T. *Tackling Sexual Violence at Universities: An International Perspective*. Routledge; 2019.

116. Women and equalities committee, house of commons. Sexual harassment of women and girls in public places: Women's safety at university [Internet]. 2018 Oct [cited 2020 Dec 10]. Available from: https://publications.parliament.uk/pa/cm201719/cmselect/cmwomeq/701/70110.htm.

117. Smith G. Hidden marks: A study of women students' experiences of harassment, stalking, violence and sexual assault. 2010. Available from: www.nusconnect.org.uk/resources/hidden-marks-a-study-of-women-students-experiences-of-harassment-stalking-violence-and-sexual-assault.

118. Kimble M, Neacsiu AD, Flack WF, Horner J. Risk of unwanted sex for college women: Evidence for a red zone. *J Am Coll Health*. 2008;57(3):331–8.

119. National Union of students. Power in the academy: Staff sexual misconduct in UK higher education [Internet]. 2018. Available from: https://web.unican.es/unidades/igualdad/SiteAssets/guia-de-recursos/acoso/NUS_staff-student_misconduct_report.pdf.

120. Jackson C, Sundaram V. *Lad Culture in Higher Education: Sexism, Sexual Harassment and Violence*. Routledge; 2020. 241 p.

121. Murnen SK, Kohlman MH. Athletic participation, fraternity membership, and sexual aggression among college men: A meta-analytic review. *Sex Roles*. 2007;57(1–2):145–57.

122. Cowan S, Munro VE. Seeking campus justice: Challenging the 'criminal justice drift' in United Kingdom university responses to student sexual violence and misconduct. *J Law Soc*. 2021;48(3):308–33.

123. Humphreys CJ, Towl GJ. *Addressing Student Sexual Violence in Higher Education: A Good Practice Guide* [Internet]. Emerald Group Publishing; 2020. Available from: https://books.google.co.uk/books?hl=en&lr=&id=LpveDwAAQBAJ&oi=fnd&pg=PP1&dq=Addressing+Student+Sexual+Violence+in+Higher+Education:+A+Good+Practice+Guide&ots=9LgFQ9rWEE&sig=panK-MrLeevFXEDn6g9T-QwhU-E#v=onepage&q=Addressing%20Student%20Sexual%20Violence%20in%20Higher%20Education%3A%20A%20Good%20Practice%20Guide&f=false.

124. Zellick G. *Committee of Vice-Chancellors and Principals of the Universities of the United Kingdom*. Final report of the Task Force on Student Disciplinary Procedures [Internet]. Place of Publication Not Identified: Publisher Not Identified; 1994. Available from: https://books.google.co.uk/books/about/Final_Report_of_the_Task_Force_on_Studen.html?id=e-uhtgAACAAJ&redir_esc=y.

125. Universities UK. Changing the culture: Report of the universities UK taskforce examining violence against women, harassment and hate crime affecting university students [Internet]. 2016 [cited 2021 Jan 12]. Available from: www.universitiesuk.ac.uk/policy-and-analysis/reports/Pages/changing-the-culture-final-report.aspx.

126. The 1752 group [Internet]. The 1752 group [cited 2021 Jan 12]. Available from: https://1752group.com/.

127. Office for students. Evaluation of safeguarding students catalyst fund projects round three – final report [Internet]. 2020. Available from: www.officeforstudents.org.uk/media/c9cbf68d-023d-4bca-bc84-095fdc8ca8c3/catalyst-round-three-summative-report.pdf.

128. Batty D, Hall R. UCL to ban intimate relationships between staff and their students. *The Guardian* [Internet]. 2020 Feb 20 [cited 2021 Aug 26]. Available from: www.theguardian.com/education/2020/feb/20/ucl-to-ban-intimate-relationships-between-staff-and-students-univesities.

129. Waymack A, Van Loan C. *Report of the Consensual Relationship Policy Committee* [Internet]. Cornell University; 2018. Available from: https://cpb-us-e1.wpmucdn.com/blogs.cornell.edu/dist/3/6798/files/2018/05/Report-CRPC-1l7gcwn.pdf.

130. Johnson PA, Widnall SE, Frazier BF. *Sexual Harassment of Women: Climate, Culture, and Consequences in Academic Sciences, Engineering, and Medicine* [Internet]. National Academies Press; 2018. Available from: www.nap.edu/read/24994/chapter/1.

131. Oman S, Bull A. Joining up well-being and sexual misconduct data and policy in HE: 'To stand in the gap' as a feminist approach. *Sociol Rev.* 2021 Oct 4;00380261211049024.

132. Hodari AK, Cunnigham B, Martinez-Miranda LJ, Urry M, Coble K, Freeland E, et al. *Many Steps Forward, a Few Steps Back: Women in Physics in the US.* Batavia, IL: Fermi National Accelerator Lab (FNAL); 2011. Report No.: FERMILAB-CONF-11–837.

133. Carter P, Jeffs T. *A Very Private Affair: Sexual Exploitation in Higher Education.* Education Now Books; 1995.

134. Whitley L, Page T. Sexism at the centre: Locating the problem of sexual harassment. *New Form.* 2015;86(86):34–53.

135. Bull A, Rye R. *Silencing Students: Institutional Responses to Staff Sexual Misconduct in Higher Education* [Internet]. Portsmouth, UK: The 1752 Group/ University of Portsmouth; 2018. Available from: https://researchportal.port.ac.uk/portal/files/11631036/Silencing_Students_The_1752_Group.pdf.

136. Revolt sexual assault, the student room. Sexual violence at university [Internet]. 2018. Available from: https://revoltsexualassault.com/wp-content/uploads/2018/03/Report-Sexual-Violence-at-University-Revolt-Sexual-Assault-The-Student-Room-March-2018.pdf.

137. Women and equalities committee, house of commons. The role of minister for women and equalities and the place of GEO in government inquiry [Internet]. 2018 Jun [cited 2021 Mar 26]. Available from: https://publications.parliament.uk/pa/cm201719/cmselect/cmwomeq/356/35604.htm#footnote-037.

138. Office for students. Statement of expectations for preventing and addressing harassment and sexual misconduct affecting students in higher education [Internet]. 2021. Available from: www.officeforstudents.org.uk/media/d4ef58c0-db7c-4fc2-9fae-fcb94b38a7f3/ofs-statement-of-expectations-harassment-and-sexual-misconduct.pdf.

139. DeGue S, Valle LA, Holt MK, Massetti GM, Matjasko JL, Tharp AT. A systematic review of primary prevention strategies for sexual violence perpetration. *Aggress Violent Behav.* 2014;19(4):346–62.

140. Ellsberg M, Ullman C, Blackwell A, Hill A, Contreras M. What works to prevent adolescent intimate partner and sexual violence? A global review of best practices. *Adolesc Dating Violence.* 2018;381–414.

141. OFSTED. Review of sexual abuse in schools and colleges [Internet]. 2021 Jun [cited 2021 Jun 11]. Available from: www.gov.uk/government/publications/review-of-sexual-abuse-in-schools-and-colleges/review-of-sexual-abuse-in-schools-and-colleges.

142. Sinozich S, Langton L. *Rape and Sexual Assault Among College-Age Females, 1995–2013* [Internet]. U.S Department of Justice; 2014. Report No.: NCJ 248471. Available from: https://bjs.ojp.gov/content/pub/pdf/rsavcaf9513.pdf.

143. Macintyre S, Ellaway A, Cummins S. Place effects on health: How can we conceptualise, operationalise and measure them? *Soc Sci Med.* 2002;55(1):125–39.

144. Ford JL, Browning CR. Neighborhoods and infectious disease risk: Acquisition of chlamydia during the transition to young adulthood. *J Urban Health.* 2014;91(1):136–50.

145. Elkin M. *Domestic Abuse: Findings from the Crime Survey for England and Wales: Year Ending March 2018* [Internet]. Office for National Statistics; 2018 Mar. Available from: www.ons.gov.uk/peoplepopulationandcommunity/crimeandjustice/articles/domes ticabusefindingsfromthecrimesurveyforenglandandwales/yearendingmarch2018# groups-of-people-most-likely-to-be-victims-of-domestic-abuse.

146. Jewkes R, Morrell R. Sexuality and the limits of agency among South African teenage women: Theorising femininities and their connections to HIV risk practises. *Soc Sci Med.* 2012;74(11):1729–37.

147. Pinchevsky GM, Wright EM. The impact of neighborhoods on intimate partner violence and victimization. *Trauma Violence Abuse.* 2012;13(2):112–32.

148. Connell RW. *Masculinities.* Cambridge: Polity Press; 1995.

149. Lorimer K, McMillan L, McDaid L, Milne D, Russell S, Hunt K. Exploring masculinities, sexual health and wellbeing across areas of high deprivation in Scotland: The depth of the challenge to improve understandings and practices. *Health Place.* 2018;50:27–41.

150. Levenson JS, Willis GM, Prescott DS. Adverse childhood experiences in the lives of male sex offenders: Implications for trauma-informed care. *Sex Abuse.* 2016;28(4):340–59.

151. Public health Scotland PH. Adverse childhood experiences (ACEs) [Internet]. 2020 [cited 2020 Dec 10]. Available from: www.healthscotland.scot/population-groups/ children/adverse-childhood-experiences-aces/overview-of-aces.

152. Heilman B, Hebert L, Paul-Gera N. *The Making of Sexual Violence: How Does a Boy Grow Up to Commit Rape? Evidence from Five IMAGES Countries* [Internet]. Washington, DC: International Centre for Research on Women/ Promundo; 2014. Available from: https://promundoglobal.org/wp-content/uploads/2014/12/The-Making-of-Sexual-Violence-How-Does-a-Boy-Grow-Up-to-Commit-Rape.pdf.

153. McDaid L, Ross G, Young I. *Men, Deprivation and Sexual Health: Scoping Review.* MRC/CSO Social and Public Health Sciences Unit; 2012.

154. Phipps A. Rape and respectability: Ideas about sexual violence and social class. *Sociology.* 2009;43(4):667–83.

155. Hill AL, Miller E, Switzer GE, Yu L, Heilman B, Levtov RG, et al. Harmful masculinities among younger men in three countries: Psychometric study of the man box scale. *Prev Med.* 2020;139:106185.

156. Bedera N, Nordmeyer K. An inherently masculine practice: Understanding the sexual victimization of queer women. *J Interpers Violence.* 2020;0886260519898439.

157. Bates L. *Everyday Sexism* [Internet]. Macmillan; 2016 [cited 2021 Aug 27]. Available from: https://us.macmillan.com/everydaysexism/laurabates/9781250100184.

158. Bronfenbrenner U. Ecological systems theory. In: Vasta R, editor. *Six Theories of Child Development: Revised Formulations and Current Issues.* Jessica Kingsley Publishers; 1992.

159. Dahlgren G, Whitehead M. *European Strategies for Tackling Social Inequities in Health: Levelling Up Part 2* [Internet]. WHO Regional office for Europe Copenhagen; 2006. Available from: www.euro.who.int/__data/assets/pdf_file/0018/103824/E89384.pdf.

160. End violence against women coalition (SPP0096). Street harassment of women and girls in public places inquiry (SPP0096) [Internet]. 2018 [cited 2021 Jan 14]. Available from: http://data.parliament.uk/writtenevidence/committeeevidence.svc/evidence document/women-and-equalities-committee/sexual-harassment-of-women-and-girls-in-public-places/written/81597.html.

161. Depraetere J, Vandeviver C, Beken TV, Keygnaert I. Big boys don't cry: A critical interpretive synthesis of male sexual victimization. *Trauma Violence Abuse.* 2020;21(5):991–1010.

162. NSPCC national society for the prevention of cruelty to children. *Statistics Briefing: Child Sexual Abuse* [Internet]. NSPCC; 2021 Mar. Available from: https://learning. nspcc.org.uk/media/1710/statistics-briefing-child-sexual-abuse.pdf.

163. Zurbriggen EL, Collins RL, Lamb S, Roberts T-A, Tolman DL, Ward LM, et al. *Report of the APA Task Force on the Sexualization of Girls* [Internet]. American Psychological Association; 2007. p. 72. Available from: www.apa.org/pi/women/programs/girls/report-full.pdf.

164. Member of the public. Street harassment of women and girls in public places inquiry (SPP0053) [Internet]. 2018 [cited 2021 Jan 8]. Available from: http://data.parliament. uk/WrittenEvidence/CommitteeEvidence.svc/EvidenceDocument/Women%20 and%20Equalities/Sexual%20harassment%20of%20women%20and%20girls%20 in%20public%20places/written/79689.html.

165. Women and equalities committee, house of commons. Sexual harassment and sexual violence in schools [Internet]. 2016 Sep [cited 2021 Jan 14]. Available from: https://publications.parliament.uk/pa/cm201617/cmselect/cmwomeq/91/9105. htm#_idTextAnchor009.

166. Dines G. *Pornland: How Porn Has Hijacked Our Sexuality*. Beacon Press; 2010.

167. Renold E. Boys and girls speak out: A qualitative study of children's gender and sexual cultures (ages 10–12). 2013. Available from: https://calio.dspacedirect.org/handle/11212/1279.

168. Lamb S, Koven J. Sexualization of girls: Addressing criticism of the APA report, presenting new evidence. *SAGE Open*. 2019 Oct 1;9(4):2158244019881024.

169. Plan international UK. Sexual harassment in the Workplace inquiry (SPP0071) [Internet]. 2018 [cited 2021 Jan 14]. Available from: http://data.parliament.uk/WrittenEvidence/CommitteeEvidence.svc/EvidenceDocument/Women%20and%20Equalities/Sexual%20harassment%20of%20women%20and%20girls%20in%20public%20places/written/79639.html.

170. ASBAE. Sexual harassment and sexual violence in schools inquiry (SVS0017) [Internet]. 2016 [cited 2021 Jan 14]. Available from: http://data.parliament.uk/writtenevidence/committeeevidence.svc/evidencedocument/women-and-equalities-committee/sexual-harassment-and-sexual-violence-in-schools/written/33189.html.

171. Holdsworth E, Trifonova V, Tanton C, Kuper H, Datta J, Macdowall W, et al. Sexual behaviours and sexual health outcomes among young adults with limiting disabilities: Findings from third British national survey of sexual attitudes and lifestyles (Natsal-3). *BMJ Open*. 2018;8(7):e019219.

172. Casteel C, Martin SL, Smith JB, Gurka KK, Kupper LL. National study of physical and sexual assault among women with disabilities. *Inj Prev*. 2008 Apr 1;14(2):87–90.

173. McGilloway C, Smith D, Galvin R. Barriers faced by adults with intellectual disabilities who experience sexual assault: A systematic review and meta-synthesis. *J Appl Res Intellect Disabil*. 2020;33(1):51–66.

174. Anti bullying alliance, national children's bureau (SVS0018). Sexual harassment and sexual violence in schools inquiry (SVS0018) [Internet]. 2016 [cited 2021 Jan 14]. Available from: http://data.parliament.uk/writtenevidence/committeeevidence.svc/evidencedocument/women-and-equalities-committee/sexual-harassment-and-sexual-violence-in-schools/written/33302.html.

175. Hillberg T, Hamilton-Giachritsis C, Dixon L. Review of meta-analyses on the association between child sexual abuse and adult mental health difficulties: A systematic approach. *Trauma Violence Abuse*. 2011 Jan 1;12(1):38–49.

176. Wekerle C, Hébert M, Daigneault I, Fortin-Langelier E, Smith S. Chapter 6 – ACEs, sexual violence, and sexual health. In: Asmundson GJG, Afifi TO, editors. *Adverse Childhood Experiences* [Internet]. Academic Press; 2020 [cited 2021 Jun 16]. p. 91–118. Available from: www.sciencedirect.com/science/article/pii/B9780128160657000069.

177. Member of the public. Street harassment of women and girls in public places inquiry (SPP0089) [Internet]. 2018 [cited 2021 Jan 14]. Available from: http://data. parliament.uk/WrittenEvidence/CommitteeEvidence.svc/EvidenceDocument/ Women%20and%20Equalities/Sexual%20harassment%20of%20women%20and%20 girls%20in%20public%20places/written/79885.html.

178. Chakraborti N, Garland J. Reconceptualizing hate crime victimization through the lens of vulnerability and 'difference'. *Theor Criminol.* 2012 Nov 1;16(4):499–514.

179. Love G, De Michele G, Giakoumidaki C, Sánchez EH, Lukera M, Cartei V. Improving access to sexual violence support for marginalised individuals: Findings from the lesbian, gay, bisexual and trans* and the black and minority ethnic communities. *Crit Radic Soc Work.* 2017;5(2):163–79.

180. Faith Matters. *Interim Report 2018: Gendered Anti-Muslim Hatred and Islamophobia* [Internet]. Faith Matters; 2018 Nov [cited 2021 Jan 21]. Available from: https://tellmamauk. org/gendered-anti-muslim-hatred-and-islamophobia-street-based-aggression-in-cases-reported-to-tell-mama-is-alarming/.

181. Purple Drum. *I'd Just Like to Be Free* [Internet]. Imkaan: End Violence Against Women; 2016 [cited 2021 Jan 14]. Available from: www.endviolenceagainstwomen.org.uk/ powerful-new-film-black-women-speak-out-about-racist-sexual-harassment/.

182. Davis J. 'Where are the Black girls in our CSA services, studies and statistics?' [Internet]. *Community Care.* 2019 [cited 2021 Feb 5]. Available from: www.com munitycare.co.uk/2019/11/20/where-are-the-black-girls-in-our-services-studies-and-statistics-on-csa/.

183. Thiara R, Roy S. *Reclaiming Voice: Minoritised Women and Sexual Violence Key Findings* [Internet]. Imkaan: University of Warwick; 2020 [cited 2020 Dec 10]. Available from: www.imkaan.org.uk/reclaiming-voice.

184. Washington PA. Disclosure patterns of Black female sexual assault survivors. *Violence Women.* 2001;7(11):1254–83.

185. Maier SL. "I have heard horrible stories . . ." Rape victim advocates' perceptions of the revictimization of rape victims by the police and medical system. *Violence Women.* 2008;14(7):786–808.

186. Long L, Ullman SE. The impact of multiple traumatic victimization on disclosure and coping mechanisms for Black women. *Fem Criminol.* 2013;8(4):295–319.

187. Gómez JM, Gobin RL. Black women and girls & #MeToo: Rape, cultural betrayal, & healing. *Sex Roles.* 2020 Jan 1;82(1):1–12.

188. Robertson HA, Nagaraj NC, Vyas AN. Family violence and child sexual abuse among South Asians in the US. *J Immigr Minor Health.* 2016;18(4):921–7.

189. Fritz N, Malic V, Paul B, Zhou Y. Worse than objects: The depiction of black women and men and their sexual relationship in pornography. *Gend Issues.* 2021;38(1):100–20.

190. Jacobs MS. The violent state: Black women's invisible struggle against police violence. *Wm Mary J Women L.* 2017;24:39.

191. Imkaan. From survival to sustainability: Critical issues for the specialist black and 'minority ethnic' ending violence against women and girls sector in the UK [Internet]. 2018 [cited 2020 Dec 10]. Available from: https://829ef90d-0745-49b2-b404-cbea85f15fda.filesusr.com/ugd/2f475d_9cab044d7d25404d85da289b70978237.pdf.

192. Rehal M, Maguire S. *The Price of Honour: Exploring the Issues of Sexual Violence Within South Asian Communities in Coventry* [Internet]. Coventry Rape and Sexual Abuse Centre; 2014. Available from: www.crasac.org.uk/uploads/2/1/6/0/21603882/the_price_of_honour_full_report.pdf.

193. End violence against women coalition. Women living in a hostile environment [Internet]. 2018 May. Available from: www.endviolenceagainstwomen.org.uk/wp-content/uploads/FINAL-living-in-a-hostile-environment-for-Web-and-sharing-.pdf.

194. Refugee council. *The Vulnerable Women's Project: Refugee and Asylum Seeking Women Affected by Rape or Sexual Violence Literature Review* [Internet]. The British Library; 2009 Feb [cited 2021 Jan 21]. Available from: www.bl.uk/collection-items/vulnerable-womens-project-refugee-and-asylum-seeking-women-affected-by-rape-or-sexual-violence-literature-review.

195. Thiara R, Roy S, Ng P. *Between the Lines: Service Responses to Black and Minority Ethnic (BME) Women and Girls Experiencing Sexual Violence*. Lond Imkaan University Warwick; 2015.

196. VOSCUR. Sexual violence needs assessment for Avon and somerset [Internet]. 2018 Apr. Available from: www.voscur.org/system/files/Needs%20Assessment_0.pdf.

197. Kanyeredzi A. *Race, Culture, and Gender: Black Female Experiences of Violence and Abuse*. Springer; 2018.

198. Heilman B, Barker G, Harrison A. *The Man Box: A Study on Being a Young Man in the US, UK, and Mexico* [Internet]. Washington, DC: Unilever/Promundo-US; 2017. Available from: https://promundoglobal.org/wp-content/uploads/2017/03/TheManBox-Full-EN-Final-29.03.2017-POSTPRINT.v3-web.pdf.

199. Page D, Whitt S. Confronting wartime sexual violence: Public support for survivors in Bosnia. *J Confl Resolut*. 2020 Apr 1;64(4):674–702.

200. Stripe N. *Sexual Offences Prevalence and Trends, England and Wales* [Internet]. Office for National Statistics; 2021 Mar [cited 2021 Mar 22]. Available from: www.ons.gov.uk/peoplepopulationandcommunity/crimeandjustice/articles/sexualoffencesprevalenceandtrendsenglandandwales/yearendingmarch2020.

201. Reed R, Pamlanye JT, Truex HR, Murphy-Neilson MC, Kunaniec KP, Newins AR, et al. Higher rates of unacknowledged rape among men: The role of rape myth acceptance. *Psychol Men Masculinities*. 2020;21(1):162.

202. Spruin L, Reilly L. An exploration into the acceptance of male rape myths within the UK. *J Forensic Sci Crim Investig*. 2018;9(3).

203. Jackson E. #USVA2017 Why men may not tell anyone they have been raped. It can "shatter their masculinity "Elton Jackson. https://t.co/djHPWnfVyu [Internet]. 2017 [cited 2021 Jan 22]. Available from: https://twitter.com/DrJaneMeyrick/status/938135718001545216.

204. Petter O. Male rape survivor speaks out about his ordeal. *The Independent* [Internet]. 2017 Jul 21 [cited 2021 Jan 22]. Available from: www.independent.co.uk/life-style/male-rape-victim-sexual-attackers-free-no-conviction-psychological-impact-men-victims-a7853311.html.

205. Brooks-Hay O, Burman M, Bradley L, Kyle D. Evaluation of the rape crisis Scotland national advocacy project. *Final Rep*. 2018;50.

206. Barker G. Male violence or patriarchal violence? Global trends in men and violence. *Sex Salud Soc Rio Jan*. 2016;316–30.

207. Kerr E, Cottee C, Chowdhury R, Jawad R, Welch J. The Haven: A pilot referral centre in London for cases of serious sexual assault. *BJOG Int J Obstet Gynaecol*. 2003;110(3):267–71.

208. Zilkens RR, Smith DA, Kelly MC, Mukhtar SA, Semmens JB, Phillips MA. Sexual assault and general body injuries: A detailed cross-sectional Australian study of 1163 women. *Forensic Sci Int*. 2017;279:112–20.

209. Jina R, Thomas LS. Health consequences of sexual violence against women. *Best Pract Res Clin Obstet Gynaecol*. 2013;27(1):15–26.

210. Werner GG, Riemann D, Ehring T. Fear of sleep and trauma-induced Insomnia: A review and conceptual model. *Sleep Med Rev*. 2020;55:101383.

211. Cadman L, Waller J, Ashdown-Barr L, Szarewski A. Barriers to cervical screening in women who have experienced sexual abuse: An exploratory study. *J Fam Plann Reprod Health Care*. 2012;38(4):214–20.

212. Rothbaum BO, Foa EB, Riggs DS, Murdock T, Walsh W. A prospective examination of post-traumatic stress disorder in rape victims. *J Trauma Stress*. 1992;5(3):455–75.

213. Feeny NC, Foa EB, Treadwell KR, March J. Posttraumatic stress disorder in youth: A critical review of the cognitive and behavioral treatment outcome literature. *Prof Psychol Res Pract*. 2004;35(5):466.

214. Dworkin ER, Schumacher JA. Preventing posttraumatic stress related to sexual assault through early intervention: A systematic review. *Trauma Violence Abuse*. 2018;19(4):459–72.

215. Ullman SE, Relyea M, Peter-Hagene L, Vasquez AL. Trauma histories, substance use coping, PTSD, and problem substance use among sexual assault victims. *Addict Behav*. 2013 Jun 1;38(6):2219–23.

216. Kessler RC, Aguilar-Gaxiola S, Alonso J, Benjet C, Bromet EJ, Cardoso G, et al. Trauma and PTSD in the WHO world mental health surveys. *Eur J Psychotraumatology*. 2017 Oct 27;8(sup5):1353383.

217. Armour C, Elklit A, Lauterbach D, Elhai JD. The DSM-5 dissociative-PTSD subtype: Can levels of depression, anxiety, hostility, and sleeping difficulties differentiate between dissociative-PTSD and PTSD in rape and sexual assault victims? *J Anxiety Disord*. 2014 May 1;28(4):418–26.

218. Busch FN. The influence of neuroscience on the theory and approaches to panic disorder and the impact of trauma. *Psychoanal Inq*. 2019 Nov 17;39(8):571–81.

219. NUS. Sexual violence in further education a study of students' experiences and perceptions of sexual harassment, violence and domestic abuse in further education [Internet]. 2019 Jun. Available from: https://feweek.co.uk/wp-content/uploads/2019/06/June-Report-Sexual-Violence-in-FE.pdf.

220. Khalifeh H, Moran P, Borschmann R, Dean K, Hart C, Hogg J, et al. Domestic and sexual violence against patients with severe mental illness. *Psychol Med*. 2015;45(4):875–86.

221. Grounded with Louis Theroux, Series 2.11. Michaela Coel [Internet]. *BBC*; 2020 [cited 2020 Dec 10]. Available from: www.bbc.co.uk/programmes/p08ybstk.

222. Potter LC, Morris R, Hegarty K, Garcia-Moreno C, Feder G. Categories and health impacts of intimate partner violence in the world health organization multi-country study on women's health and domestic violence. *Int J Epidemiol*. 2020;1:11.

223. Smith PH, White JW, Holland LJ. A longitudinal perspective on dating violence among adolescent and college-age women. *Am J Public Health*. 2003;93(7):1104–9.

224. Roberge EM, Bryan CJ. An integrated model of chronic trauma-induced insomnia. *Clin Psychol Psychother*. 2021;28(1):79–92.

225. Dolsen MR, Asarnow LD, Harvey AG. Insomnia as a transdiagnostic process in psychiatric disorders. *Curr Psychiatry Rep* [Internet]. 2014 [cited 2021 Feb 11];16(471). Available from: https://link.springer.com/article/10.1007/s11920-014-0471-y.

226. Steine IM, Harvey AG, Krystal JH, Milde AM, Grønli J, Bjorvatn B, et al. Sleep disturbances in sexual abuse victims: A systematic review. *Sleep Med Rev.* 2012 Feb 1;16(1):15–25.

227. Basile KC, Smith SG, Chen J, Zwald M. Chronic diseases, health conditions, and other impacts associated with rape victimization of US women. *J Interpers Violence.* 2020;0886260519900335.

228. Jewkes R, Sen P, Garcia-Moreno C. *Sexual Violence* [Internet]. WHO; 2002. Available from: www.who.int/violence_injury_prevention/violence/world_report/en/full_en.pdf?ua=1.

229. Member of the public. Street harassment of women and girls in public places inquiry (SPP008) [Internet]. 2018 [cited 2021 Feb 25]. Available from: http://data.parliament.uk/WrittenEvidence/CommitteeEvidence.svc/EvidenceDocument/Women%20and%20Equalities/Sexual%20harassment%20of%20women%20and%20girls%20in%20public%20places/written/76790.html.

230. The Bristol street harassment project [Internet]. Bristol zero tolerance is a BWV project. 2018 [cited 2021 Feb 12]. Available from: www.bristolzerotolerance.com/take-action/take-action-as-an-individual/.

231. Vera-Gray F. *The Right Amount of Panic: How Women Trade Freedom for Safety.* Policy Press; 2018.

232. Amnesty international UK. UK: New poll finds a third of people believe women who flirt partially responsible for being raped [Internet]. 2005 [cited 2021 Feb 12]. Available from: www.amnesty.org.uk/press-releases/uk-new-poll-finds-third-people-believe-women-who-flirt-partially-responsible-being.

233. Ruddick G. Have I got news for you where jo brand rebuked all-male panel tops complaints. *The Guardian* [Internet]. 2017 Nov 16 [cited 2021 Feb 12]. Available from: www.theguardian.com/media/2017/nov/16/have-i-got-news-for-you-where-jo-brand-rebuked-all-male-panel-tops-complaints.

234. Member of the public. Street harassment of women and girls in public places inquiry (SPP008) [Internet]. 2018. Available from: http://data.parliament.uk/WrittenEvidence/CommitteeEvidence.svc/EvidenceDocument/Women%20and%20Equalities/Sexual%20harassment%20of%20women%20and%20girls%20in%20public%20places/written/76842.html.

235. Bos AL, Greenlee JS, Holman MR, Oxley ZM, Lay JC. This one's for the boys: How gendered political socialization limits girls' political ambition and interest. *Am Polit Sci Rev.* 2021;1–18.

236. Gueta K, Eytan S, Yakimov P. Between healing and revictimization: The experience of public self-disclosure of sexual assault and its perceived effect on recovery. *Psychol Violence.* 2020;10(6):626–37.

237. Torielli J. Psychoeducation: Discussing trauma with patients. In: Ades V, editors. *Sexual and Gender-Based Violence* [Internet]. Springer; 2020. p. 19–36. Available from: https://doi.org/10.1007/978-3-030-38345-9_2.

238. Rapalyea T. What do I say? How to support survivors | Boston area rape crisis center [Internet]. 2018 [cited 2021 Feb 25]. Available from: https://barcc.org/blog/details/what-do-i-say-how-to-support-survivors.

239. Van der Kolk BA. The body keeps the score: Memory and the evolving psychobiology of posttraumatic stress. *Harv Rev Psychiatry.* 1994;1(5):253–65.

240. Meyrick J, Anning A. *It's About Getting Your Life Back: Evaluation of Justice Groups* [Internet]. University of the West of England; 2021. Available from: unpublished.

241. McGlynn C, Westmarland N. Kaleidoscopic justice: Sexual violence and victim-survivors' perceptions of justice. *Soc Leg Stud*. 2019;28(2):179–201.

242. Williamson E, Eisenstadt N, Hester M. Justice, inequalities, and gender based violence (GBV): Victim-survivor (VS) perspectives. In: *Poster*. Friedberg; 2019.

243. Warrington C, Ackerley E, Beckett H, Walker M, Allnock D. *Making Noise: Children's Voices for Positive Change After Sexual Abuse* [Internet]. University of Bedfordshire/Office of Children's Commissioner; 2016. Available from: www.beds.ac.uk/media/86813/makingnoise-20042017.pdf.

244. Mogulescu K. Legal systems and needs: Considerations for survivors of gender-based violence. In: Ades V, editors. *Sexual and Gender-Based Violence* [Internet]. Springer; 2020. p. 233–56. Available from: https://doi.org/10.1007/978-3-030-38345-9_13.

245. Kunst M, Popelier L, Varekamp E. Victim satisfaction with the criminal justice system and emotional recovery: A systematic and critical review of the literature. *Trauma Violence Abuse*. 2015 Jul 1;16(3):336–58.

246. Smith O. Cultural scaffolding and the long view of rape trials. In: *Sexual Violence on Trial* [Internet]. Routledge; 2021. Available from: www.taylorfrancis.com/chapters/edit/10.4324/9780429356087-25/cultural-scaffolding-long-view-rape-trials-olivia-smith.

247. Heydon G, Powell A. Written-response interview protocols: An innovative approach to confidential reporting and victim interviewing in sexual assault investigations. *Polic Soc*. 2018 Jul 24;28(6):631–46.

248. Kilmartin C, Allison J. *Men's Violence Against Women: Theory, Research, and Activism* [Internet]. Psychology Press; 2007. Available from: www.taylorfrancis.com/books/mono/10.4324/9780203937136/men-violence-women-christopher-kilmartin-julie-allison?refId=32420118-be7c-41fa-82d1-4e613e13d3fd.

249. Crown prosecution service. *Violence Against Women and Girls Report 2018–19* [Internet]. CPS; 2019 [cited 2021 Mar 11]. Available from: www.cps.gov.uk/sites/default/files/documents/publications/cps-vawg-report-2019.pdf.

250. Swartout KM, Swartout AG, Brennan CL, White JW. Trajectories of male sexual aggression from adolescence through college: A latent class growth analysis. *Aggress Behav*. 2015;41(5):467–77.

251. Gervais SJ, DiLillo D, McChargue D. Understanding the link between men's alcohol use and sexual violence perpetration: The mediating role of sexual objectification. *Psychol Violence*. 2014;4(2):156.

252. Serisier T. Sex crimes and the media. *Oxf Res Encycl Criminol* [Internet]. 2017 Jan 25 [cited 2021 Mar 12]. Available from: https://oxfordre.com/criminology/view/10.1093/acrefore/9780190264079.001.0001/acrefore-9780190264079-e-118.

253. Cuklanz L. Media representation of rape and sexual assault. *Int Encycl Gend Media Commun*. 2020;1–5.

254. Keren R. The language of gender violence [Internet]. *Jackson Katz*. 2012 [cited 2021 Jun 30]. Available from: www.jacksonkatz.com/news/language-gender-violence/.

255. Meager T. *The Danger of the Monster Myth: What Men Can Do to End Violence Against Women and Promote Gender Equality* [Internet]. White Ribbon Ireland; 2014 [cited 2020 Dec 15]. Available from: https://whiteribbonblog.com/2014/04/17/the-danger-of-the-monster-myth/.

256. McCartan K. Current understandings of paedophilia and the resulting crisis in modern society. *Psychol Sex Dysfunct*. 2008;51–84.

257. McCartan K. *Responding to Sexual Offending: Perceptions, Risk Management and Public Protection*. Springer; 2014. 248 p.

258. Casey EA, Masters T. Sexual violence risk and protective factors: A systematic review of the literature [Internet]. 2017. Available from: www.doh.wa.gov/Portals/1/Documents/Pubs/140-164-SexualViolenceRiskProtectiveFactors.pdf.

259. Kahn RE, Jackson K, Keiser K, Ambroziak G, Levenson JS. Adverse childhood experiences among sexual offenders: Associations with sexual recidivism risk and psychopathology. *Sex Abuse*. 2020;1079063220970031.

260. Murnen SK, Wright C, Kaluzny G. If "boys will be boys," then girls will be victims? A meta-analytic review of the research that relates masculine ideology to sexual aggression. *Sex Roles*. 2002;46(11):359–75.

261. Blumenthal S. Violence as communication. *Crim Justice Matters*. 2006;66(1):4–5.

262. Kilmartin C. Counseling men to prevent sexual violence. In: *A Counselor's Guide to Working with Men* [Internet]. American Counseling Association Alexandria, VA; 2014. p. 247–62. Available from: https://books.google.co.uk/books?hl=en&lr=&id=g-z2tBQAAQBAJ&oi=fnd&pg=PA247&dq=Counseling+men+to+prevent+sexual+violence&ots=cV3dskDWS3&sig=2enOHJq_uSAa7xOuCyE834MXVeo&redir_esc=y#v=onepage&q=Counseling%20men%20to%20prevent%20sexual%20violence&f=false.

263. Tsitsika A, Critselis E, Kormas G, Konstantoulaki E, Constantopoulos A, Kafetzis D. Adolescent pornographic internet site use: A multivariate regression analysis of the predictive factors of use and psychosocial implications. *Cyberpsychol Behav*. 2009;12(5):545–50.

264. Plan international, UK. Street harassment of women and girls in public places inquiry (SPP0099) [Internet]. 2018 [cited 2021 Mar 12]. Available from: http://data.parliament.uk/WrittenEvidence/CommitteeEvidence.svc/EvidenceDocument/Women%20and%20Equalities/Sexual%20harassment%20of%20women%20and%20girls%20in%20public%20places/written/82791.html.

265. Peter J, Valkenburg PM. Adolescents and pornography: A review of 20 years of research. *J Sex Res*. 2016;53(4–5):509–31.

266. Vera-Gray F, McGlynn C, Kureshi I, Butterby K. Sexual violence as a sexual script in mainstream online pornography. *Br J Criminol* [Internet]. 2021 Apr 4 [cited 2021 Apr 6];(azab035). Available from: https://doi.org/10.1093/bjc/azab035.

267. Sacks M, Ackerman AR, Shlosberg A. Rape myths in the media: A content analysis of local newspaper reporting in the United States. *Deviant Behav*. 2018 Sep 2;39(9):1237–46.

268. Willmott D, Boduszek D, Booth N. The English jury on trial. *Custod Rev*. 2017;82:12–14.

269. Fulu E, Warner X, Miedema S, Jewkes R, Roselli T, Lang J. *Why Do Some Men Use Violence Against Women and How Can We Prevent It? Quantitative Findings from the United Nations Multi-Country Study on Men and Violence in Asia and the Pacific* [Internet]. UNDP, UNFPA, UN Women, UNV; 2013. Available from: https://g.co/kgs/TEkBmz.

270. Heilman B, Barker G. *Masculine Norms and Violence: Making the Connections* [Internet]. Promundo-US; 2018. Available from: https://promundoglobal.org/wp-content/uploads/2018/04/Masculine-Norms-and-Violence-Making-the-Connection-20180424.pdf.

271. Stanaland A, Gaither S. "Be a man": The role of social pressure in eliciting men's aggressive cognition. *Pers Soc Psychol Bull*. 2021 Jan 27;0146167220984298.

272. Stratmoen E, Greer MM, Martens AL, Saucier DA. What, I' m not good enough for you? Individual differences in masculine honor beliefs and the endorsement of aggressive responses to romantic rejection. *Personal Individ Differ*. 2018;123:151–62.

273. Berdahl JL. The sexual harassment of uppity women. *J Appl Psychol*. 2007;92(2):425–37.

274. Stanko E. *Intimate Intrusions (Routledge Revivals): Women's Experience of Male Violence*. Routledge; 2013.

275. Vignoles VL. Identity motives. In: *Handbook of Identity Theory and Research*. Springer; 2011. p. 403–32.

276. Breakwell GM. *Coping with Threatened Identities*. Psychology Press; 2015.

277. Jaspal R. Social psychological debates about identity. In: Jaspal R, Breakwell GM, editors. *Identity Process Theory: Identity, Social Action and Social Change* [Internet]. 2014 [cited 2021 Mar 19]. Available from: https://books.google.co.uk/books?hl=en&lr=&id=GL8d AwAAQBAJ&oi=fnd&pg=PA3&ots=QfDQH8tsNS&sig=iBio-w-JEciMsg 9FmE93KK2vZOI&redir_esc=y#v=onepage&q&f=false.

278. Davis SN, Blake A. Does biology limit equality? In: Risman BJ, Froyum CM, Scarborough WJ, editors. *Handbook of the Sociology of Gender* [Internet]. Cham: Springer International Publishing; 2018 [cited 2021 Jul 22]. p. 109–18 (Handbooks of Sociology and Social Research). Available from: https://doi.org/10.1007/978-3-319-76333-0_8.

279. Angier N. *Woman-An Intimate Geography Houghton*. Anchor; 1999.

280. Caldwell MF. Quantifying the decline in juvenile sexual recidivism rates. *Psychol Public Policy Law*. 2016;22(4):414.

281. Thompson MP, Swartout KM, Koss MP. Trajectories and predictors of sexually aggressive behaviors during emerging adulthood. *Psychol Violence*. 2013 Jul 1;3(3):247–59.

282. Thompson MP, Kingree JB, Zinzow H, Swartout K. Time-varying risk factors and sexual aggression perpetration among male college students. *J Adolesc Health*. 2015;57(6):637–42.

283. Bates L. *Men Who Hate Women: From Incels to Pickup Artists, the Truth About Extreme Misogyny and How It Affects Us All*. Simon and Schuster; 2020. 410 p.

284. Messerschmidt JW. Adolescent boys, embodied heteromasculinities and sexual violence. *Cent Educ Policy Stud J*. 2017;7(2):113–26.

285. Lorimer K, McMillan L, McDaid L, Milne D, Russell S, Hunt K. Exploring masculinities, sexual health and wellbeing across areas of high deprivation in Scotland: The depth of the challenge to improve understandings and practices. *Health Place*. 2018;50:27–41.

286. Quinn BA. Sexual harassment and masculinity: The power and meaning of "girl watching". *Gend Soc*. 2002;16(3):386–402.

287. Clark L. The trouble with boys: What lies behind the flood of teenage sexual assault stories? [Internet]. *The Guardian*. 2021 [cited 2021 Mar 11]. Available from: www.theguardian.com/society/2021/feb/27/the-trouble-with-boys-what-lies-behind-the-flood-of-teenage-sexual-assault-stories.

288. Bragg S, Renold E, Ringrose J, Jackson C. 'More than boy, girl, male, female': Exploring young people's views on gender diversity within and beyond school contexts. *Sex Educ*. 2018;18(4):420–34.

289. Kilmartin C. *The Fictions That Shape Men's Lives*. Routledge; 2021.

290. Ragnoese C, Shand T, Barker G. *Masculine Norms and Men's Health: Making the Connections* [Internet]. Promundo-US; 2019. Available from: https://promundoglobal.org/wp-content/uploads/2019/02/Masculine-Norms-Mens-Health-Report_007_Web.pdf.

291. Promundo-US. *Manhood 2.0: Program Overview and Final Results* [Internet]. Washington, DC; 2019 [cited 2021 Mar 11]. Available from: https://promundoglobal.org/resources/manhood-2-0-curriculum/?lang=english.

292. Bonilla-Silva E. *Racism Without Racists: Color-Blind Racism and the Persistence of Racial Inequality in the United States*. Rowman & Littlefield Publishers; 2006.

293. United Nations, general assembly. Declaration on the elimination of violence against women 48/104 [Internet]. Dec 20, 1993. Available from: www.un.org/en/genocidepre vention/documents/atrocity-crimes/Doc.21_declaration%20elimination%20vaw.pdf.

294. GQ TE. What 1,147 Men think about #MeToo: A glamour x GQ survey. GQ [Internet]. 2018 [cited 2021 Jun 17]. Available from: www.gq.com/story/metoo-and-men-survey-glamour-gq.

295. Fawcett society, Hogan Lovells. #Metoo one year on – what's changed? [Internet]. 2018 Oct [cited 2021 Mar 18]. Available from: www.fawcettsociety.org.uk/Handlers/Download.ashx?IDMF=8709c721-6d67-4d1f-8e30-11347c56a7c5.

296. Stöckl H, Quigg Z. Violence against women and girls. *BMJ*. 2021 Aug 6;374:n1926.

297. Sen P, Borges U, Guallar E, Cochran J. *Towards and End to Sexual Harassment: The Urgency and Nature of Change in the Era of #MeToo* [Internet]. UN Women; 2018. Available from: www.unwomen.org/en/digital-library/publications/2018/11/towards-an-end-to-sexual-harassment#view.

298. Lanthier S, Du Mont J, Mason R. Responding to delayed disclosure of sexual assault in health settings: A systematic review. *Trauma Violence Abuse*. 2018;19(3):251–65.

299. Ullman SE, Peter-Hagene L. Social reactions to sexual assault disclosure, coping, perceived control, and PTSD symptoms in sexual assault victims. *J Community Psychol*. 2014;42(4):495–508.

300. UN women. *The Shadow Pandemic: Violence Against Women During COVID-19* [Internet]. UN Women; 2020 [cited 2021 Oct 7]. Available from: www.unwomen.org/en/news/in-focus/in-focus-gender-equality-in-covid-19-response/violence-against-women-during-covid-19.

301. Koss MP. Detecting the scope of rape: A review of prevalence research methods. *J Interpers Violence*. 1993;8(2):198–222.

302. Starzynski LL, Ullman SE, Filipas HH, Townsend SM. Correlates of women's sexual assault disclosure to informal and formal support sources. *Violence Vict*. 2005;20(4):417–32.

303. Atkin V. Sexual harassment of women and girls in public places inquiry (Q261) [Internet]. 2018 [cited 2021 Apr 6]. Available from: http://data.parliament.uk/writtenevi dence/committeeevidence.svc/evidencedocument/women-and-equalities-committee/sexual-harassment-of-women-and-girls-in-public-places/oral/86537.html.

304. Cantor D, Fisher B, Chibnall S, Townsend R, Lee H, Bruce C, et al. *AAU Climate Survey on Sexual Assault and Sexual Misconduct*. Association of American Universities; 2015. Available from: www. aau. edu/uploadedFiles. . . .

305. Smith D, Letourneau EJ, Saunders BE, Kilpatrick DG, Resnick HS, Best CL. Delay in disclosure of childhood rape: Results from a national survey. *Child Abuse Negl*. 2000;24(2):273–87.

306. Stanton S. *A Qualitative and Quantitative Analysis of Empirical Data on Violence Against Women in Greater Cape Town from 1989 to 1991*. Institute of Criminology, University of Cape Town; 1993.

307. Higson-Sweeney N, Meyrick J. "Who could help me? There was nothing. I brought it on myself": A qualitative study exploring UK university student experiences of sexual violence. *PsyPAG Q*. 2022;122.

308. Wilson LC, Miller KE. Meta-analysis of the prevalence of unacknowledged rape. *Trauma Violence Abuse*. 2016;17(2):149–59.

309. Peterson ZD, Muehlenhard CL. A match-and-motivation model of how women label their nonconsensual sexual experiences. *Psychol Women Q*. 2011 Dec 1;35(4):558–70.

310. Möller A, Söndergaard HP, Helström L. Tonic immobility during sexual assault – a common reaction predicting post-traumatic stress disorder and severe depression. *Acta Obstet Gynecol Scand.* 2017;96(8):932–8.

311. Centre for women's justice, end violence against women coalition, Imkaan, rape crisis England & Wales. The decriminalisation of rape: Why the justice system is failing rape survivors and needs to change [Internet]. 2020 [cited 2020 Dec 11]. Available from: https://rapecrisis.org.uk/media/2396/c-decriminalisation-of-rape-report-cwj-evaw imkaan-rcew-nov-2020.pdf.

312. TeBockhorst SF. *I Still Have to Overcome Just Being Captured Inside Myself: The Experience and Meaning of Peritraumatic Tonic Immobility Among Survivors of Sexual Violence.* University of Northern Colorado 2012;265.

313. Ahrens CE, Campbell R, Ternier-Thames NK, Wasco SM, Sefl T. Deciding whom to tell: Expectations and outcomes of rape survivors' first disclosures. *Psychol Women Q.* 2007;31(1):38–49.

314. Lessing JE. Primary care provider interventions for the delayed disclosure of adolescent sexual assault. *J Pediatr Health Care.* 2005;19(1):17–24.

315. End violence against women coalition. Attitudes to sexual consent research for the end violence against women coalition by YouGov [Internet]. 2018. Available from: www.endviolenceagainstwomen.org.uk/wp-content/uploads/1-Attitudes-to-sexual-consent-Research-findings-FINAL.pdf.

316. Taaffe H. *Sounds Familiar – Reveals Hostility, Complacency and a Blame Culture Against Women* [Internet]. Fawcett Society; 2017 [cited 2020 Dec 10]. Available from: www. fawcettsociety.org.uk/sounds-familiar.

317. Yapp EJ, Quayle E. A systematic review of the association between rape myth acceptance and male-on-female sexual violence. *Aggress Violent Behav.* 2018;41:1–19.

318. Stanko E. Warnings to women: Police advice and women's safety in Britain [Internet]. 1996 [cited 2021 Sep 22]. Available from: https://journals.sagepub.com/doi/abs/10.1177/1077801296002001002.

319. Grierson J. Sarah Everard case: People stopped by lone officer could 'wave down a bus', says met. *The Guardian* [Internet]. 2021 Oct 1 [cited 2021 Oct 8]. Available from: www.theguardian.com/uk-news/2021/oct/01/police-must-win-back-public-confidence-after-sarah-everard-case-says-minister.

320. Crown prosecution service. Rape and serious sexual offences (RASSO) 2025 [Internet]. 2020 [cited 2021 Jan 7]. Available from: www.cps.gov.uk/publication/rape-and-serious-sexual-offences-rasso-2025.

321. Ahrens CE, Janna S, Jennings A. To tell or not to tell: The impact of disclosure on sexual assault survivors' recovery. *Violence Vict.* 2010;25(5):631–48.

322. Coy M, Tyler M. 5 Pornographication and heterosexualisation in public space. *Contentious Cities Des Gendered Prod Space.* 2020;49.

323. Bows H, Herring J. Getting away with murder? A review of the 'rough sex defence'. *J Crim Law.* 2020;84(6):525–38.

324. Carroll JS, Padilla-Walker LM, Nelson LJ, Olson CD, McNamara Barry C, Madsen SD. Generation XXX: Pornography acceptance and use among emerging adults. *J Adolesc Res.* 2008;23(1):6–30.

325. Cowell A, Smith E. *Streetwise Pornography Research.* Newcastle Tyne Streetwise Young People's Project; 2009.

326. Bridges AJ, Wosnitzer R, Scharrer E, Sun C, Liberman R. Aggression and sexual behavior in best-selling pornography videos: A content analysis update. *Violence Women.* 2010;16(10):1065–85.

327. Carrotte ER, Davis AC, Lim MS. Sexual behaviors and violence in pornography: Systematic review and narrative synthesis of video content analyses. *J Med Internet Res.* 2020;22(5):e16702.

328. Jensen R. Why porn? Why this porn? Why so little concern? [Internet]. *Merion West.* 2021 [cited 2021 Jun 28]. Available from: https://merionwest.com/2021/06/24/why-porn-why-this-porn-why-so-little-concern/.

329. Berelowitz S, Firmin C, Edwards G, Gulyurtlu S. *I Thought I Was the Only One. The Only One in the World: Child Sexual Exploitation in Gangs and Groups.* Interim Rep Office for the Children's Commissoner England; 2012.

330. Häggström-Nordin E, Sandberg J, Hanson U, Tydén T. 'It's everywhere!' Young Swedish people's thoughts and reflections about pornography. *Scand J Caring Sci.* 2006;20(4):386–93.

331. Davis A, Carrotte ER, Hellard ME, Lim MS. What behaviors do young heterosexual Australians see in pornography? A cross-sectional study. *J Sex Res.* 2018;55(3):310–9.

332. Crabbe M, Flood M. School-based education to address pornography's influence on young people: A proposed practice framework. *Am J Sex Educ.* 2021;1–46.

333. Charles P, Meyrick J. Exploring the way sexually explicit material informs sexual beliefs, understanding and practices of young men: A qualitative survey. *J Health Psychol.* 2020;25(13–14):2211–21.

334. Wright PJ. Pornography and sexual behavior: Do sexual attitudes mediate or confound? *Commun Res.* 2020 Apr 1;47(3):451–75.

335. Upton J, Hazell A, Abbott R, Pilling K. *The Relationship Between Pornography Use and Harmful Sexual Attitudes and Behaviours* [Internet]. Government Equalities Office; 2020 Feb. Available from: https://assets.publishing.service.gov.uk/government/uploads/system/uploads/attachment_data/file/976730/The_Relationship_between_Pornography_use_and_Harmful_Sexual_Attitudes_and_Behaviours-_literature_review_v1.pdf.

336. Barr C, Topping A. Fewer than one in 60 rape cases lead to charge in England and Wales. *The Guardian* [Internet]. 2021 May 23 [cited 2021 May 24]. Available from: www.theguardian.com/society/2021/may/23/fewer-than-one-in-60-cases-lead-to-charge-in-england-and-wales.

337. HM government. The end-to-end rape review report on findings and actions [Internet]. 2021 Jun p. 68. Available from: https://assets.publishing.service.gov.uk/government/uploads/system/uploads/attachment_data/file/994816/end-to-end-rape-review-report.pdf.

338. Baird V. CPS statistics show a further drop in rape charges despite police referring more cases – victims commissioner [Internet]. 2020 [cited 2020 Dec 10]. Available from: https://victimscommissioner.org.uk/news/cps-statistics-show-a-further-drop-in-rape-charges-despite-police-referring-more-cases/.

339. Smith O, Skinner T. Observing court responses to victims of rape and sexual assault. *Fem Criminol.* 2012;7(4):298–326.

340. Crown prosecution service. Rape and sexual offences – Chapter 4: Tackling rape myths and stereotypes. In: *The Code for Crown Prosecutors* [Internet]. 2021 [cited 2021 Sep 22]. Available from: www.cps.gov.uk/legal-guidance/rape-and-sexual-offences-chapter-4-tackling-rape-myths-and-stereotypes.

341. Judicial college. Crown court bench book: Directing the jury first supplement [Internet]. 2011. Available from: www.judiciary.uk/wp-content/uploads/JCO/Documents/eLetters/CCBB_first_supplement_071211.pdf.

342. Bongiorno R, Langbroek C, Bain PG, Ting M, Ryan MK. Why women are blamed for being sexually harassed: The effects of empathy for female victims and male perpetrators. *Psychol Women Q.* 2020;44(1):11–27.

343. Ortberg M. CNN reports on the 'promising future' of the Steubenville rapists, who are very good students [Internet]. *Gawker.* 2013 [cited 2021 Mar 22]. Available from: http://gawker.com/5991003/cnn-reports-on-the-promising-future-of-the-steuben-ville-rapists-who-are-very-good-students.

344. Topping A. Scrap juries in rape trials, labour MP suggests. *The Guardian* [Internet]. 2018 Nov 21 [cited 2021 Mar 25]. Available from: www.theguardian.com/society/2018/nov/21/scrap-juries-in-rape-trials-labour-mp-ann-coffey.

345. Lisak D, Gardinier L, Nicksa SC, Cote AM. False allegations of sexual assault: An analysis of ten years of reported cases. *Violence Women.* 2010;16(12):1318–34.

346. Kitching C. Girls, 15, 'raped at Australian resort' after meeting 3 men on New Year's Eve. *Mirror* [Internet]. 2021 Jan 1 [cited 2021 Sep 22]. Available from: www.mirror.co.uk/news/world-news/two-girls-15-raped-holiday-23249264.

347. Kelly L, Temkin J, Griffiths S. *Section 41: An Evaluation of New Legislation Limiting Sexual History Evidence in Rape Trials.* Home Office London; 2006.

348. McGlynn C. Rape trials and sexual history evidence: Reforming the law on third-party evidence. *J Crim Law.* 2017 Oct 1;81(5):367–92.

349. Lippman JR. I did it because I never stopped loving you: The effects of media portrayals of persistent pursuit on beliefs about stalking. *Commun Res.* 2018;45(3):394–421.

350. Norris S. Systemic failings mean most rapists can attack women with impunity [Internet]. *Byline Times.* 2020 [cited 2020 Dec 16]. Available from: https://bylinetimes.com/2020/12/16/systemic-failings-mean-most-rapists-can-attack-women-with-impunity/.

351. McKenzie-Mohr S, Lafrance MN. Telling stories without the words: 'Tightrope talk' in women's accounts of coming to live well after rape or depression. *Fem Psychol.* 2011;21(1):49–73.

352. Jeffrey NK, Barata PC. The intersections of normative heterosexuality and sexual violence: University men's talk about sexual behavior in intimate relationships. *Sex Roles.* 2020 Sep 1;83(5):353–69.

353. Carrie P. *Being Boys: Being Girls: Learning Masculinities and Femininities: Learning Masculinities and Femininities.* McGraw-Hill Education; 2007. 189 p.

354. NUS. That's what she said: Women students' experiences of 'lad culture' in higher education [Internet]. 2013. Available from: http://sro.sussex.ac.uk/id/eprint/49011/1/That's_what_she_said_full_report_Final_web.pdf.

355. Weiss KG. "Boys will be boys" and other gendered accounts: An exploration of victims' excuses and justifications for unwanted sexual contact and coercion. *Violence Women.* 2009 Jul 1;15(7):810–34.

356. Flood M. Men and# metoo: Mapping Men's responses to anti-violence advocacy. In: *# MeToo and the Politics of Social Change.* Springer; 2019. p. 285–300.

357. Winton T. About the boys: Tim Winton on how toxic masculinity is shackling men to misogyny. *The Guardian* [Internet]. 2018 Apr 9 [cited 2021 Jun 24]. Available from: www.theguardian.com/books/2018/apr/09/about-the-boys-tim-winton-on-how-toxic-masculinity-is-shackling-men-to-misogyny.

358. Member of the public. Street harassment of women and girls in public places inquiry (SPP0029) [Internet]. 2018 [cited 2020 Dec 10]. Available from: http://data.parliament.uk/WrittenEvidence/CommitteeEvidence.svc/EvidenceDocument/

Women%20and%20Equalities/Sexual%20harassment%20of%20women%20and%20 girls%20in%20public%20places/written/77543.html.

359. Fitzgerald LF, Gelfand MJ, Drasgow F. Measuring sexual harassment: Theoretical and psychometric advances. *Basic Appl Soc Psychol*. 1995 Dec 1;17(4):425–45.

360. Aycock LM, Hazari Z, Brewe E, Clancy KBH, Hodapp T, Goertzen RM. Sexual harassment reported by undergraduate female physicists. *Phys Rev Phys Educ Res*. 2019 Apr 22;15(1):010121.

361. Fish S. Street harassment of women and girls in public places inquiry (SPP0056) [Internet]. 2018 [cited 2020 Dec 15]. Available from: http://data.parliament.uk/ WrittenEvidence/CommitteeEvidence.svc/EvidenceDocument/Women%20 and%20Equalities/Sexual%20harassment%20of%20women%20and%20girls%20 in%20public%20places/written/79590.html.

362. Associated Press. In wake of Weinstein, men wonder if hugging women still OK | *Daily Mail Online*. 2017 Dec 4 [cited 2020 Dec 15]. Available from: www.dailymail. co.uk/news/article-5144997/In-wake-Weinstein-men-wonder-hugging-women-OK.html.

363. Dent G. A note to men worried about #MeToo [Internet]. *Women's Agenda*. 2018 [cited 2021 Jan 7]. Available from: https://womensagenda.com.au/latest/a-note-to-men-worried-about-metoo/.

364. Clancy KBH, Cortina LM, Kirkland AR. Opinion: Use science to stop sexual harassment in higher education. *Proc Natl Acad Sci*. 2020 Sep 15;117(37):22614–8.

365. Jozkowski KN, Peterson ZD, Sanders SA, Dennis B, Reece M. Gender differences in heterosexual college students' conceptualizations and indicators of sexual consent: Implications for contemporary sexual assault prevention education. *J Sex Res*. 2014;51(8):904–16.

366. Muehlenhard CL, Humphreys TP, Jozkowski KN, Peterson ZD. The complexities of sexual consent among college students: A conceptual and empirical review. *J Sex Res*. 2016;53(4–5):457–87.

367. Holmström C, Plantin L, Elmerstig E. Complexities of sexual consent: Young people's reasoning in a Swedish context. *Psychol Sex*. 2020 Oct 1;11(4):342–57.

368. Peterson ZD, Muehlenhard CL. Conceptualizing the "wantedness" of women's consensual and nonconsensual sexual experiences: Implications for how women label their experiences with rape. *J Sex Res*. 2007;44(1):72–88.

369. Brady G, Lowe P, Brown G, Osmond J, Newman M. 'All in all it is just a judgement call': Issues surrounding sexual consent in young people's heterosexual encounters. *J Youth Stud*. 2018 Jan 2;21(1):35–50.

370. Baldwin-White A. "When a girl says no, you should be persistent until she says yes": College students and their beliefs about consent – *Adrienne Baldwin-White, 2021*. 2019 [cited 2021 Sep 23]. Available from: https://journals.sagepub.com/doi/ abs/10.1177/0886260519875552.

371. Austen J. Pride and prejudice: A novel in three volumes. In: Egerton T, editors. *Military Library*. Whitehall; 1813.

372. Jozkowski KN, Hunt M. Who wants a quitter? . . . So you just keep trying": How college students' perceptions of sexual consent privilege men. In: *Annual Meeting of the Society for the Scientific Study of Sexuality*. Omaha, Nebraska; 2014.

373. Stratmoen E, Rivera ED, Saucier DA. "Sorry, I already have a boyfriend": Masculine honor beliefs and perceptions of women's use of deceptive rejection behaviors to avert unwanted romantic advances. *J Soc Pers Relatsh*. 2020 Feb 1;37(2):467–90.

374. Hester M, Mulvihill N, Matolcsi A, Sanchez AL, Walker S-J. *The Nature and Prevalence of Prostitution and Sex Work in England and Wales Today* [Internet]. University of Bristol; 2019. Available from: https://assets.publishing.service.gov.uk/government/uploads/sys tem/uploads/attachment_data/file/842920/Prostitution_and_Sex_Work_Report.pdf.

375. O'Neil A, Sojo V, Fileborn B, Scovelle AJ, Milner A. The# MeToo movement: An opportunity in public health? *The Lancet*. 2018;391(10140):2587–9.

376. McCartan K, Kemshall H, Tabachnick J. The construction of community understandings of sexual violence: Rethinking public, practitioner and policy discourses. *J Sex Aggress*. 2015;21(1):100–16.

377. Bellis MA, Hughes K, Perkins C, Bennett A. *Protecting People, Promoting Health: A Public Health Approach to Violence Prevention for England*. Public Health England; 2012.

378. Advertising standards authority, committees of advertising practice. Depictions, perceptions and harm: A report on gender stereotypes in advertising summary report [Internet]. 2017 [cited 2021 Apr 28]. Available from: www.asa.org.uk/asset/FA0CDD1A-6453-42FF-BD2892D70C53C5E7/.

379. Harrington C, Neilson T. A review of research on sexual violence in audio-visual media [Internet]. 2009. Available from: www.classificationoffice.govt.nz/assets/PDFs/review-of-research-on-sexual-violence-2009.pdf.

380. Merken S, James V. Perpetrating the myth: Exploring media accounts of rape myths on "women's" networks. *Deviant Behav*. 2020 Sep 1;41(9):1176–91.

381. Williams Z. From line of duty to the fall: Why can't TV shows stop killing women? *The Guardian* [Internet]. 2021 Mar 18 [cited 2021 Apr 30]. Available from: www.theguardian.com/tv-and-radio/2021/mar/18/from-line-of-duty-to-the-fall-why-cant-tv-shows-stop-killing-women.

382. Triboit P. Spiral – Series 1: Episode 1 [Internet]. 2005 [cited 2021 Apr 30]. Available from: www.bbc.co.uk/iplayer/episode/b0074sk6/spiral-series-1-episode-1.

383. Wainwright S. Happy valley [Internet]. 2014. Available from: http://downloads.bbc.co.uk/writersroom/scripts/happy-valley-ep6.pdf.

384. Jermyn D. Silk blouses and fedoras: The female detective, contemporary TV crime drama and the predicaments of postfeminism. *Crime Media Cult*. 2017 Dec 1;13(3):259–76.

385. Malling S, Asbæk P, August P. *Efterforskningen. Miso Film, TV2, Outline Film*; 2021.

386. BARB | Broadcasters audience research board [Internet] [cited 2021 Jun 24]. Available from: www.barb.co.uk/.

387. Cavender G, Bond-Maupin L, Jurik NC. The construction of gender in reality crime TV. *Gend Soc*. 1999;13(5):643–63.

388. Dodd V, Sherwood H. Two met police officers arrested over photo of murdered sisters. *The Guardian* [Internet]. 2020 Jun 25 [cited 2021 May 13]. Available from: www.theguardian.com/uk-news/2020/jun/25/two-met-police-officers-arrested-over-photo-of-murdered-sisters.

389. Anonymous. Personal Communication with Crime Drama Producer. 2021.

390. World health organization. RESPECT women preventing violence against women [Internet]. 2019. Available from: https://apps.who.int/iris/bitstream/handle/10665/312261/WHO-RHR-18.19-eng.pdf?ua=1.

391. Fulu E. A summary of the evidence and research agenda for what works: A global programme to prevent violence against women and girls [Internet]. 2014 [cited 2021 Apr 1]. Available from: https://assets.publishing.service.gov.uk/government/uploads/system/uploads/attachment_data/file/337599/summary-evidence-research-agenda-C.pdf.

392. Kettrey HH, Marx RA. The effects of bystander programs on the prevention of sexual assault across the college years: A systematic review and meta-analysis. *J Youth Adolesc.* 2019;48(2):212–27.

393. Law commission. Hate crime: Background to our review [Internet]. 2019 p. 12. Available from: https://s3-eu-west-2.amazonaws.com/lawcom-prod-storage-11jsxou 24uy7q/uploads/2019/07/6.5286-LC_Hate-Crime_Information-Paper_A4_ FINAL_030719_WEB.pdf.

394. Wellstead A, Cairney P, Oliver K. Reducing ambiguity to close the science-policy gap. *Policy Des Pract.* 2018 Apr 3;1(2):115–25.

395. Gibbs A, Washington L, Abdelatif N, Chirwa E, Willan S, Shai N, et al. Stepping stones and creating futures intervention to prevent intimate partner violence among young people: Cluster randomized controlled trial. *J Adolesc Health.* 2020 Mar 1;66(3):323–35.

396. Knight L, Ranganathan M, Abramsky T, Polzer-Ngwato T, Muvhango L, Molebatsi M, et al. Intervention with microfinance for AIDS and gender equity (IMAGE): Women's engagement with the scaled-up IMAGE programme and experience of intimate partner violence in rural South Africa. *Prev Sci.* 2020 Feb 1;21(2):268–81.

397. Ruane-McAteer E, Gillespie K, Amin A, Aventin Á, Robinson M, Hanratty J, et al. Gender-transformative programming with men and boys to improve sexual and reproductive health and rights: A systematic review of intervention studies. *BMJ Glob Health.* 2020 Oct 1;5(10):e002997.

398. Kerr-Wilson A, Gibbs A, McAslan Fraser E, Ramsoomar L, Parke A, Khuwaja HMA, et al. What works to prevent violence among women and girls: A rigorous global evidence review of interventions to prevent violence against women and girls [Internet]. 2020. Available from: www.whatworks.co.za/documents/ publications/374-evidence-reviewfweb/file.

399. Dobbin F, Kalev A. Why sexual harassment programs backfire. *Harvard Business Review* [Internet]. 2020 May 1 [cited 2021 Mar 26]. Available from: https://hbr.org/2020/05/ why-sexual-harassment-programs-backfire.

400. Kidder DL, Lankau MJ, Chrobot-Mason D, Mollica KA, Friedman RA. Backlash toward diversity initiatives: Examining the impact of diversity program justification, personal and group outcomes. *Int J Confl Manag.* 2004;15(1):77–102.

401. Bondestam F, Lundqvist M. Sexual harassment in higher education – a systematic review. *Eur J High Educ.* 2020 Oct 1;10(4):397–419.

402. Men and Violence [Internet]. Woman's hour. 2021 [cited 2021 Apr 9]. Available from: www.bbc.co.uk/programmes/m000t6kt.

403. Bailey ZD, Krieger N, Agénor M, Graves J, Linos N, Bassett MT. Structural racism and health inequities in the USA: Evidence and interventions. *The Lancet.* 2017 Apr 8;389(10077):1453–63.

404. Commission on race and ethnic disparities. Commissionon race and ethnic disparities: The report [Internet]. 2021 Mar. Available from: www.gov.uk/government/ publications/the-report-of-the-commission-on-race-and-ethnic-disparities.

405. Action aid. Common cause, collaborative response: Violence against women and girls and reproductive health and rights [Internet]. 2017. Available from: www.actionaid. org.uk/sites/default/files/publications/actionaid-familyplanning-report.pdf.

406. Member of the public. Street harassment of women and girls in public places inquiry (SPP0077) [Internet]. 2018 [cited 2021 Apr 8]. Available from: http://data.parliament. uk/WrittenEvidence/CommitteeEvidence.svc/EvidenceDocument/Women%20

and%20Equalities/Sexual%20harassment%20of%20women%20and%20girls%20
in%20public%20places/written/79669.html.

407. Olusoga D. David Olusoga: His Edinburgh television festival speech in full. *The Guardian* [Internet]. 2020 Aug 24 [cited 2021 Mar 25]. Available from: www.theguardian.com/media/2020/aug/24/david-olusoga-his-edinburgh-television-festival-speech-in-full.

408. Osbourne L, Barnett J, Blackwood L. "You never feel so Black as when you're contrasted against a White background": Black students' experiences at a predominantly white institution in the UK. *J Community Appl Soc Psychol* [Internet]. 2021 [cited 2021 Apr 6];n/a(n/a). Available from: https://onlinelibrary.wiley.com/doi/abs/10.1002/casp.2517.

409. King TL, Kavanagh A, Scovelle AJ, Milner A. Associations between gender equality and health: A systematic review. *Health Promot Int.* 2020 Feb 1;35(1):27–41.

410. Wilbur K, Snyder C, Essary AC, Reddy S, Will KK, Mary Saxon. Developing workforce diversity in the health professions: A social justice perspective. *Health Prof Educ.* 2020 Jun 1;6(2):222–9.

411. Tinkler JE. How do sexual harassment policies shape gender beliefs? An exploration of the moderating effects of norm adherence and gender. *Soc Sci Res.* 2013 Sep 1;42(5):1269–83.

412. Yates D. Quick fixes won't stop sexual harassment in academia, experts say [Internet]. *PhysOrg.* 2020 [cited 2021 Apr 9]. Available from: https://phys.org/news/2020-08-quick-wont-sexual-academia-experts.html.

413. Istanbul convention. Oral evidence [Internet]. Sect. International Agreements Select Committee Feb 2021. Available from: https://committees.parliament.uk/oralevidence/1687/pdf/.

414. Medeiros K, Griffith J. #Ustoo: How I-O psychologists can extend the conversation on sexual harassment and sexual assault through workplace training. *Ind Organ Psychol.* 2019 Mar;12(1):1–19.

415. Office for national statistics. Gender pay gap in the UK – Office for national statistics [Internet]. 2020 [cited 2021 Mar 26]. Available from: www.ons.gov.uk/employmentandlabourmarket/peopleinwork/earningsandworkinghours/bulletins/genderpaygapintheuk/2020.

416. Kaur S. *Sex & Power 2020* [Internet]. Fawcett Society; 2020 Jan. Available from: www.fawcettsociety.org.uk/Handlers/Download.ashx?IDMF=bdb30c2d-7b79-4b02-af09-72d0e25545b5.

417. International Centre for research on women. Gender equity and male engagement: It only works when everyone plays [Internet]. 2018. Available from: www.icrw.org/publications/gender-equity-male-engagement/.

418. The convention on the elimination of all forms of discrimination against women (CEDAW) inquiry [Internet]. Sect. Women and Equalities Committee Nov 14, 2018. Available from: www.parliamentlive.tv/Event/Index/8efe4547-e9df-4e1a-9d43-d8120b186e5e.

419. Women and equalities committee, house of commons. Enforcing the equality act: The law and the role of the equality and human rights commission: Tenth report of session 2017–19 [Internet]. 2019 Jul [cited 2021 Apr 6]. Report No.: HC 1470. Available from: https://publications.parliament.uk/pa/cm201919/cmselect/cmwomeq/96/9602.htm.

420. Rizzo TA, Stevanovic-Fenn N, Smith G, Glinski AM, O'Brien-Milne L, Gammage S. *The Costs of Sex-Based Harassment to Business: An in-Depth Look at the Workplace.* International Centre for Research on Women (ICRW); 2018.

421. Birchall J, Edstrom J, Shahrokh T. *Reframing Men and Boys in Policy for Gender Equality* [Internet]. IDS, Sonke Gender Justice, Promundo; 2016 Mar. Available from: https://promundoglobal.org/resources/emerge-policy-brief-reframing-men-and-boys-in-policy-for-gender-equality/?lang=english.

422. Edström J, Shahrokh T. *Reframing Men and Boys in Policy for Gender Equality: Conceptual Guidance and an Agenda for Change.* IDS, Sonke Gender Justice, Promundo; 2016.

423. Fileborn B. Bystanders often don't intervene in sexual harassment – but should they? *The Conversation* [Internet]. 2017 Feb 20 [cited 2021 Apr 29]. Available from: http://theconversation.com/bystanders-often-dont-intervene-in-sexual-harassment-but-should-they-72794.

424. Roden J, Mustafaj M, Saleem M. Who else likes it? Perceived gender of social endorsers predicts gender equality support. *Comput Hum Behav.* 2021;118:106696.

425. Haberland NA. The case for addressing gender and power in sexuality and HIV education: A comprehensive review of evaluation studies. *Int Perspect Sex Reprod Health.* 2015;41(1):31–42.

426. Casey E, Carlson J, Two Bulls S, Yager A. Gender transformative approaches to engaging men in gender-based violence prevention: A review and conceptual model. *Trauma Violence Abuse.* 2018 Apr 1;19(2):231–46.

427. Burrell S, Ruxton S, Westmarland N. *Changing Gender Norms: Engaging with Men and Boys.* Government Equalities Office; 2019 Oct.

428. Flood M. Men building gender equality: A guide to XY's content [Internet]. Men, masculinities and gender politics. 2018 [cited 2021 May 7]. Available from: https://xyonline.net/content/men-building-gender-equality-guide-xys-content.

429. Burrell S, Ruxton S, Westmarland N. *Engaging with Men and Boys about Gender Norms: Engagement Toolkit.* Government Equalities Office; 2020 Jan.

430. American psychological association. *APA Guidelines for Psychological Practice with Boys and Men* [Internet]. American Psychological Association; 2018 [cited 2021 May 7]. Available from: http://doi.apa.org/get-pe-doi.cfm?doi=10.1037/e505472019-001.

431. Parker S. Irvine Welsh on men, #MeToo and whether there'll be another trainspotting novel. *Esquire* [Internet]. 2018 Apr 13 [cited 2021 May 20]. Available from: www.esquire.com/uk/culture/books/a19756077/irvine-welsh-on-men-metoo-and-whether-therell-be-another-trainspotting-novel/.

432. The Men's Project, Flood M. *The Man Box: A Study on Being a Young Man in Australia – Google Search* [Internet]. Melbourne: Jesuit Social Services; 2018 [cited 2021 Apr 30]. Available from: https://apo.org.au/sites/default/files/resource-files/2018-10/apo-nid197286.pdf.

433. White Ribbon UK [Internet]. White Ribbon UK [cited 2021 May 7]. Available from: www.whiteribbon.org.uk.

434. Plan international, Promundo. 9 Tips for parents: Raising sons to embrace health, positive masculinity [Internet]. 2019. Available from: https://promundoglobal.org/wp-content/uploads/2019/06/healthy-masculinity-tipsheet-for-parents.pdf.

435. Baldwin S, Malone M, Sandall J, Bick D. Mental health and wellbeing during the transition to fatherhood: A systematic review of first time fathers' experiences. *JBI Evid Synth.* 2018 Nov;16(11):2118–91.

436. Mennicke A, Kennedy SC, Gromer J, Klem-O'Connor M. Evaluation of a social norms sexual violence prevention marketing campaign targeted toward college men: Attitudes, beliefs, and behaviors over 5 years. *J Interpers Violence.* 2021 Apr 1;36(7–8):NP3999–4021.

437. De Koker P, Mathews C, Zuch M, Bastien S, Mason-Jones AJ. A systematic review of interventions for preventing adolescent intimate partner violence. *J Adolesc Health.* 2014 Jan 1;54(1):3–13.

438. Flood M, Russell G, O'Leary J, Brown C. Men make a difference: How to engage men on gender equality, synopsis report [Internet]. 2017. Available from: www.dca. org.au/sites/default/files/dca_engaging_men_synopsis_online_final.pdf.

439. Flood M, Dragiewicz M, Pease B. Resistance and backlash to gender equality. *Aust J Soc Issues.* 2020;56(3):3930–408.

440. Nutbeam M, Mereish EH. Negative attitudes and beliefs toward the #MeToo movement on Twitter. *J Interpers Violence.* 2021 Mar 23;08862605211001470.

441. Rich MD, Utley EA, Janke K, Moldoveanu M. "I'd rather be doing something else:" Male resistance to rape prevention programs. *J Men's Stud.* 2010;18(3):268–88.

442. PettyJohn ME, Muzzey FK, Maas MK, McCauley HL. HowIWillChange: Engaging men and boys in the #MeToo movement. *Psychol Men Masculinity.* 2019 Oct 1;20(4):612–22.

443. Folke O, Rickne J, Tanaka S, Tateishi Y. Sexual harassment of women leaders. *Daedalus.* 2020 Jan 1;149(1):180–97.

444. Jilani H. Report of Hina Jilani, special representative of the secretary-general on human rights defenders, pursuant to commission on human rights resolution 2000/61 [Internet]. United Nations; 2002 Mar [cited 2021 May 7]. Report No.: 2000/61. Available from: https://digitallibrary.un.org/record/461707.

445. Department of education. Relationships education, relationships and sex education (RSE), and health education [Internet]. 2019 [cited 2021 Apr 9]. Available from: https://assets.publishing.service.gov.uk/government/uploads/system/uploads/attachment_data/file/908013/Relationships_Education__Relationships_and_Sex_Education__RSE__and_Health_Education.pdf.

446. Tender: Acting to end abuse [Internet]. Tender [cited 2021 May 21]. Available from: https://tender.org.uk/.

447. Coker AL, Bush HM, Brancato CJ, Clear ER, Recktenwald EA. Bystander program effectiveness to reduce violence acceptance: RCT in high schools. *J Fam Violence.* 2019 Apr 1;34(3):153–64.

448. Hillman N. *Sex and Relationships Among Students: Summary Report.* Higher Education Policy Institute; 2021 p. 20. Report No.: Policy Note 30.

449. Addis S, Snowdon L. *What Works to Prevent Violence Against Women, Domestic Abuse and Sexual Violence (VAWDASV)* [Internet]. Wales Violence Prevention Unit; 2021. Available from: www.violencepreventionwales.co.uk/cms-assets/research/What-Works-to-Prevent-Violence-against-Women-Domestic-Abuse-and-Sexual-Violence-Systematic-Evidence-Assessment_2021-09-20-124755_aypz.pdf.

450. Lomax J, Meyrick J. Systematic review: Effectiveness of psychosocial interventions on wellbeing outcomes for adolescent or adult victim/survivors of recent rape or sexual assault. *J Health Psychol.* 2020;1359105320950799.

451. Meyrick J. Addressing the sexual harassment/abuse reporting gap at university: Evidence- based measures for a whole organisation approach to 'earning' disclosure from victim/survivors. unpublished. 2021.

452. Meyrick J, McCartan K, Thomas Z, Kowalska A. Barriers to sexual assault disclosure within sexual health services: A mixed method/population study. *Sex Transm Infect* [Internet]. 2019 [cited 2021 Jan 8];95(1). Available from: https://sti.bmj.com/content/95/Suppl_1/A153.1.

453. Safe dates prevention program for dating abuse – Hazelden [Internet] [cited 2021 Apr 29]. Available from: www.hazelden.org/web/public/safedates.page.

454. Shifting boundaries | Prevent IPV [Internet] [cited 2021 Apr 29]. Available from: https://preventipv.org/materials/shifting-boundaries.

455. Department for education. Sexual violence and sexual harassment between children in schools and colleges: Advice for governing bodies, proprietors, headteachers, principals, senior leadership teams and designated safeguarding leads [Internet]. 2018 May p. 44. Available from: https://assets.publishing.service.gov.uk/government/uploads/system/uploads/attachment_data/file/719902/Sexual_violence_and_sexual_harassment_between_children_in_schools_and_colleges.pdf.

456. Department for education. Keeping children safe in education (2020) Statutory guidance for schools and colleges [Internet]. 2021 p. 119. Available from: https://assets.publishing.service.gov.uk/government/uploads/system/uploads/attachment_data/file/954314/Keeping_children_safe_in_education_2020_-_Update_-_January_2021.pdf.

457. Home office. This is abuse campaign summary report [Internet]. 2015. Available from: https://assets.publishing.service.gov.uk/government/uploads/system/uploads/attachment_data/file/410010/2015-03-08_This_is_Abuse_campaign_summary_report__2_.pdf.

458. Hudspith L, Wager N, Willmott D, Gallagher B. Forty years of rape myth acceptance interventions: A systematic review of what works in naturalistic institutional settings and how this can be applied to educational guidance for jurors. *Trauma Violence Abuse.* 2021 Sep 28. https://doi.org/10.1177/15248380211050575

459. McGlynn C, Munro VE. *Rethinking Rape Law: International and Comparative Perspectives.* Routledge; 2010. 546 p.

460. Kalev A, Dobbin F, Kelly E. Best practices or best guesses? Assessing the efficacy of corporate affirmative action and diversity policies. *Am Sociol Rev.* 2006 Aug 1;71(4):589–617.

461. Bull A, Calvert-Lee G, Page T. Discrimination in the complaints process: Introducing the sector guidance to address staff sexual misconduct in UK higher education. Perspect Policy Pract High Educ. 2021 Apr 3;25(2):72–7.

462. Hazell W. Universities 'put on notice' that they could be sued over student sexual harassment. *Inews.co.uk* [Internet]. 2021 Apr 15 [cited 2021 May 20]. Available from: https://inews.co.uk/news/education/universities-put-on-notice-could-be-sued-sex-abuse-top-unis-everyones-invited-957878.

463. Feather J, Martin R, Nevile S. *Global Evidence Review of Sexual Exploitation and Abuse and Sexual Harassment (SEAH) in the Aid Sector* [Internet]. RSH Resource & Support Hub; 2021. Available from: https://gisf.ngo/resource/global-evidence-review-of-sexual-exploitation-and-abuse-and-sexual-harassment-in-the-aid-sector/.

464. International development committee, house of commons. *Progress on Tackling the Sexual Exploitation and Abuse of Aid Beneficiaries* [Internet]. House of Commons; 2021 [cited 2021 Mar 25]. Available from: https://publications.parliament.uk/pa/cm5801/cmselect/cmintdev/605/60502.htm.

465. Committee on the impacts of sexual harassment in academia. *Sexual Harassment of Women: Climate, Culture, and Consequences in Academic Sciences, Engineering, and Medicine* [Internet]. Washington, DC: National Academies Press; 2018 Aug [cited 2021 Mar 25] p. 24994. Available from: www.nap.edu or at www.nationalacademies.org/sexualharassment.

466. Harris RJ, McDonald DP, Sparks CS. Sexual harassment in the military: Individual experiences, demographics, and organizational contexts. *Armed Forces Soc.* 2018;44(1):25–43.

467. Defence Committee. Proecting those who protect us: Women in the armed forces: From recruitment to civilian life [Internet]. 2021 p. 103. Report No.: HC154. Available from: https://committees.parliament.uk/publications/6959/documents/72771/default/.

468. John Carr. Changing cultures underpinning male violence against women. *Oral Evidence* [Internet]. 2021. Available from: https://committees.parliament.uk/oralevidence/2147/default/.

469. Molloy D. Porn blocker 'missing' from online safety bill prompts concern. *BBC News* [Internet]. 2021 May 18 [cited 2021 May 21]. Available from: www.bbc.com/news/technology-57143746.

470. Kristof N. Opinion | The children of Pornhub. *The New York Times* [Internet]. 2020 Dec 4 [cited 2021 May 14]. Available from: www.nytimes.com/2020/12/04/opinion/sunday/pornhub-rape-trafficking.html.

471. Meyrick J, Higson-Sweeney N. Understanding sexual violence at University: An evidence based response. In: 2020. Available from: www.ucl.ac.uk/equality-diversity-inclusion/dignity-ucl/calling-time-sexual-misconduct.

472. Ingala Smith K. Counting dead women [Internet]. *Karen Ingala Smith*. 2019 [cited 2021 May 13]. Available from: https://kareningalasmith.com/counting-dead-women/.

473. Hollaback! Together we have the power to end harassment [Internet]. Hollaback! Together we have the power to end harassment [cited 2021 May 13]. Available from: www.ihollaback.org/.

474. It's not ok [Internet]. Child sexual exploitation it's not okay [cited 2021 May 14]. Available from: www.itsnotokay.co.uk/.

475. TIME'S UP Now. Join us [Internet]. TIME'S UP now [cited 2021 May 14]. Available from: https://timesupnow.org.

476. I will be heard [Internet]. IICSA. 2017 [cited 2021 May 14]. Available from: www.truthproject.org.uk/i-will-be-heard.

477. Holland KJ, Cortina LM. "It happens to girls all the time": Examining sexual assault survivors' reasons for not using campus supports. *Am J Community Psychol*. 2017;59(1–2):50–64.

478. 1752 Group, MCalllister Olivarius. Briefing no. 1: In cases of suspected sexual misconduct can a university pro-actively investigate and speak to potential witnesses in the absence of any formal complaint or complainant? (February 2020) 1. 2018 Sep. Report No.: 1.

479. Purna Sen [HC1335]. Changing cultures underpinning male violence against women [Internet]. 2021. Available from: https://committees.parliament.uk/oralevidence/2147/default/.

480. Clements CM, Ogle RL. Does acknowledgment as an assault victim impact postassault psychological symptoms and coping? *J Interpers Violence*. 2009 Oct 1;24(10):1595–614.

481. Rickert VI, Wiemann CM, Vaughan RD. Disclosure of date/acquaintance rape: Who reports and when. *J Pediatr Adolesc Gynecol*. 2005 Feb 1;18(1):17–24.

482. World health organization. *Responding to Intimate Partner Violence and Sexual Violence Against Women: WHO Clinical and Policy Guidelines* [Internet]. World Health Organization; 2013. 66 p. Available from: www.who.int/publications/i/item/WHO-RHR-13-10.

483. Todahl J, Walters E. Universal screening for intimate partner violence: A systematic review. *J Marital Fam Ther*. 2011;37(3):355–69.

484. Rickert VI, Edwards S, Harrykissoon SD, Wiemann CM. Violence in the lives of young women: Clinical care and management. *Curr Womens Health Rep*. 2001 Oct 1;1(2):94–101.

485. Meyrick J. So. Sexual health people. Screening for sexual abuse/ violence in sexual /reproductive healthcare. What is current practice where you work? @veroniac @ cerievans61 @lamassey1 @SARSAS_uk @doctor_oxford @BASHH_UK @FSRH_ UK @SHIPSexHealth @vanessa_apea @TheSexDoctorUK @sonaliwl [Internet]. @DrJaneMeyrick. 2021 [cited 2021 Sep 9]. Available from: https://twitter.com/ DrJaneMeyrick/status/1358733750365020161.

486. Sullivan V, de Sa J, Hamlyn E, Baraitser P. How can we facilitate online disclosure of safeguarding concerns in under 18s to support transition from online to face-to-face care? *Int J STD AIDS*. 2020 May 1;31(6):553–9.

487. Young SL, Maguire KC. Talking about sexual violence. *Women Lang WL*. 2003 Fall;26(2):40–52.

488. Kaur K, Christie C. *Cordis Bright Consulting. Local Commissioning of Services Addressing Child Sexual Abuse and Exploitation in England a Rapid Review Incorporating Findings from Five Locations*. Centre of Expertise on Child Sexual Abuse; 2018 Jan p. 56.

489. Hester M, Lilley S-J. More than support to court: Rape victims and specialist sexual violence services. *Int Rev Vict*. 2018 Sep 1;24(3):313–28.

490. Newins AR, Wilson LC, Kanefsky RZ. What's in a label? The impact of media and sexual assault characteristics on survivor rape acknowledgment. *J Trauma Stress*. 2021;34(2):405–15.

491. Ryan M. The progress and pitfalls of television's treatment of rape [Internet]. *Variety*. 2016 [cited 2021 Apr 30]. Available from: https://variety.com/2016/tv/features/ rape-tv-television-sweet-vicious-jessica-jones-game-of-thrones-1201934910/.

492. TTIE, WIF. Geena Davis foundation. Behind the scenes the state of inclusion and equity in TV writing [Internet]. 2021. Available from: https://seejane.org/wp-content/ uploads/ttie-behind-the-scenes-2021-report.pdf.

493. Jusino T. Alison Bechdel asks you to call it 'Bechdel-Wallace test' | The Mary sue [Internet]. 2015 [cited 2021 May 13]. Available from: www.themarysue.com/ bechdel-wallace-test-please-alison-bechdel/.

494. Geena Davis foundation. If he can see, it will he be it? Representations of masculinity in boys' television [Internet]. 2020. Available from: https://seejane.org/wp-content/ uploads/if-he-can-see-it-will-he-be-it-representations-of-masculinity-in-boys-tv.pdf.

495. Nottinghamshire sexual violence support service. IPSO review of editor's code – our response [Internet]. *Notts SVS Services*. 2020 [cited 2021 May 13]. Available from: https://nottssvss.org.uk/ipso-review-editors-code-response/.

496. Hirsch JS. Desire across borders: Markets, migration, and marital HIV risk in rural Mexico. *Cult Health Sex*. 2015 May 29;17(sup1):20–33.

497. Quigg Z, Bigland C, Hughes K, Duch M, Juan M. Sexual violence and nightlife: A systematic literature review. *Aggress Violent Behav*. 2020 Mar 1;51:101363.

498. Lippy C, DeGue S. Exploring alcohol policy approaches to prevent sexual violence perpetration – *Caroline Lippy, Sarah DeGue, 2016*. 2014 [cited 2021 Oct 13]. Available from: https://journals.sagepub.com/doi/full/10.1177/1524838014557291.

499. Jaffe AE, Steel AL, DiLillo D, Messman-Moore TL, Gratz KL. Characterizing sexual violence in intimate relationships: An examination of blame attributions and rape acknowledgment. *J Interpers Violence*. 2021 Jan 1;36(1–2):469–90.

500. Willis GM. Why call someone by what we don't want them to be? The ethics of labeling in forensic/correctional psychology. *Psychol Crime Law*. 2018 Aug 9;24(7):727–43.

501. Muhammad KG. *The Condemnation of Blackness – Khalil Gibran Muhammad* [Internet]. First Harvard University Press; 2010 [cited 2021 May 14]. Available from: www.hup. harvard.edu/catalog.php?isbn=9780674238145.

Index

For Product Safety Concerns and Information please contact our EU
representative GPSR@taylorandfrancis.com
Taylor & Francis Verlag GmbH, Kaufingerstraße 24, 80331 München, Germany